CW00890252

'The modern state did not build capitalism but inherited it. Sometimes it favours it, sometimes it puts obstacles in its way. At times it permits it to expand freely, but at times it destroys its resources.'

Fernand Braudel,
Civilisation and Capitalism

'If assistance so to be distributed to a certain class of people, a power must be lodged somewhere of discriminating the proper object, and of managing the concerns of the institutions that are necessary, but any great interference with the affairs of other people is a species of tyranny, and, in the common course of things, the exercise of this power may be expected to become grating to those who are driven to ask for support.'

T.R. Malthus,
Essay on Population

'The state must act by general rules. It cannot undertake to discriminate between the deserving and undeserving indigent.'

John Stuart Mill,
Principles of Political Economy

Mr J A Holborn
353 Springbank West
Hull
HU3 1LD

The May Day
Manifesto

DEFENDING THE WELFARE STATE

Mr Blair's 'Reforms'

A rolling programme of the
Independent Labour Network,
of which this is Part One

by
Michael Barratt Brown

SPOKESMAN
for the
Independent Labour Network

Published for Ken Coates MEP, on behalf of the
GUE/NGL Group in the European Parliament

First published in Great Britain in 1998 by
Spokesman
Bertrand Russell House
Gamble Street
Nottingham, England
Tel. 0115 9708318
Fax. 0115 9420433

Publications list on request

Copyright © Spokesman, 1998

This book is copyright under the Berne Convention. All rights are reserved.
Apart from any fair dealing for the purpose of private study, research, criticism
or review, as permitted under the Copyright Act, 1956, no part of this
publication may be reproduced, stored in a retrieval system, or transmitted, in
any form or by any means, electronic, electrical, chemical, mechanical,
photocopying, recording or otherwise, without the prior permission of the
copyright owner.

Enquiries should be addressed to the publishers.

British Library Cataloguing in Publication Data available on request from the
British Library.

With grateful acknowledgements to Steve Bell for permission to use
his cartoons.

ISBN 0-85124-615-X

Contents

Preface   7

Chapter 1 *Introduction and Summary*   17

Chapter 2 *The Green Paper*   24

Chapter 3 *What Mr Brown is Offering*   37

Chapter 4 *Starting from Beveridge*   50

Chapter 5 *The DSS Welfare Reform Focus Files*   56

Chapter 6 *Mr Blair's Road Show*   72

Chapter 7 *Who Pays for the Welfare State?*   78

Chapter 8 *European Comparisons*   86

Chapter 9 *What Should be Reformed*   97

Chapter 10 *Towards a New Manifesto*   103

Annexe *1. Statistical*   116
            2. Case Studies   124

Sponsors of the May Day Manifesto

Michael Barratt Brown, Derbyshire
Kate Buckell, National Union of Students Executive
David Byrne, Gateshead
Malcolm Christie, Leeds
Professor Ken Coates MEP
Professor Gerry Cohen, Oxford
Mike Davies, Leeds
Professor Ben Fine, SOAS, London
Ken Fleet, Nottingham
Celia Foote, Leeds
Dr. Jay Ginn, Guildford
Bob Holman, Glasgow
Professor Chris Jones, Liverpool
Hugh Kerr MEP
Geoff Martin, London UNISON
Professor Robert Moore, Liverpool
Jill Mountford, Welfare State Network
John Nicholson, Manchester
John Palmer, Brussels
Jimmy Reid, Glasgow
Tom Rigby, London
Professor Malcolm Sawyer, Leeds
Tony Simpson, Nottingham
Fred Twine, Aberdeen
Hilary Wainwright, Red Pepper
Jane Young, Leeds

Acknowledgements

The text is the entire responsibility of Michael Barratt Brown. He wishes to thank the following persons for their contributions and comments.

Professor Sarah Aber, Guildford
David Byrne, Gateshead
Professor Nicholas Deakin, Birmingham
Professor David Donnison, Glasgow
Ken Fleet, Nottingham
Dr Jay Ginn, Guildford
Jeff Goatcher, Hucknall
Professor Norman Ginsburg, North London
Bob Holman, Director, Easterhouse Estate, Glasgow
Richard Hopkins, Bristol
Rachel Hurst, Disability Rights
Professor Chris Jones, Liverpool
Professor Robert Moore, Liverpool
Jon O'Neill, Mansfield
John Palmer, Brussels
Professor Hilary Rose, Bradford
Professor Malcolm Sawyer, Leeds
Regan Scott, T&GWU
Tony Simpson, Nottingham
Fred Twine, Aberdeen
Professor John Veit-Wilson, Newcastle

Preface

by Ken Coates MEP & Hugh Kerr MEP

May 1st, 1998 marks the anniversary of a New Labour Government.

It also marks a more convulsive anniversary, of continuous protestations of Labour solidarity over more than a century. The first May Day in modern times was celebrated in Chicago in 1886, after the achievement of an eight hour day in some companies in that city. A very large demonstration to extend this benefit more widely was followed by days of strikes and ferocious police intimidation, culminating in mayhem, with a bomb thrown into a large contingent of policemen, and the subsequent trial and execution of a number of anarchist leaders. All this persuaded the American Federation of Labour to call for an international demonstration on the 1st May 1890. All over Britain trade unions answered this call. Thousands of working people demonstrated in every part of the country, and began a tradition of London May Day celebrations which has been observed continuously ever since. And all over Europe the same pattern established itself.

The rise and fall of fascism crushed some labour movements, and temporarily eclipsed their demonstrations. The rise and fall of communism, over a much longer period, turned some demonstrations into official parades, and removed both their spontaneity and their affirmation of alternative possibilities. But still May Day continued, and in many countries was able to insist on the possibility of an alternative society, on liberty as well as equality and fraternity.

The profound heresies of emancipation are still more than ever necessary. Mass unemployment has returned to haunt Europe, and with it have come back poverty and despair for millions of people. Unheard of riches have now been amassed to mock the poor, who are more numerous than before. The advance of invention, far from bringing freedom to wider populations, is craftily subverted into ever more sophisticated methods of manipulation and oppression. The UK has the most unequal distribution of income of any country in the European Union.

It was always honourable to stand for human freedom, and May Day offered a useful symbol of the unity of mankind and mutual support. At first sight, the election of a New Labour Government should have been a notable contribution to a continuous historical celebration.

But on this May Day we already know that New Labour confronts socialists in Britain with problems they have hardly hitherto considered. It is true that the Labour Party has always been a coalition of different forces, and that previous Labour Governments have combined different policy commitments, faltering from time to time in their pursuit of their supporters' ideals and interests. But New Labour is something else. It has explicitly abandoned a large part of the broad socialist tradition. Redistributive policies, and planned public intervention to create jobs and uphold higher social standards have now gone. Instead, the new Government defends an economic strategy based on 'the enterprise of the market and the rigour of competition', a philosophy of de-regulation, and 'a partnership with business ... that puts industry first'. It seeks 'to enhance the dynamism of the market economy, not to undermine it'. It is determined 'to extend the flexible labour markets to the rest of Europe, not to import 'Euro-sclerosis''.

These engagements are linked with a policy of less direct taxation, and refusal to 'impose burdens on business', although in fact British business bears lower taxes and makes less contributions to welfare than almost any other industrialised country.

It is within the context of stringent curbs on public expenditure that New Labour seeks to 'reform the welfare state'. Unsurprisingly, these commitments do not impress organised labour, or those non-governmental organisations which have always worked with the poor, the disabled, pensioners, or young people, nor do they impress compassionate Church people. All these social groupings know that public spending on welfare and social cohesion has suffered from prolonged neglect during the previous years of Conservative administration, and that further stringency can only mean increased hardship for many people.

As the implications of these deep policy commitments of New Labour have come home to more and more people there has been a growing sense of revulsion among 'old' Labour Party members. Many thousands of people have left the Labour Party. Others remain members, but suffer a growing sense of frustration and despair. Because the Labour leadership had aroused resistance from Labour Members of the European Parliament before the General Election, it decided to abolish the autonomy and independence of this Group. Using the pretext of their pledge to introduce proportional representation, they invented very autocratic procedures designed to impose a central discipline, with central control of the composition and numbering of the lists of candidates that would be presented in the forthcoming European Elections in 1999. Constituencies will be abolished, with the removal of the bond between elected Members and their electors. Although Party members will be allowed token participation in the nomination of candidates, the actual selections, and their crucial ordering in the lists which are presented, and which will determine who actually gets elected, will be done by the Party leadership. When these plans became clear, a number of MEPs sought to inform Labour Party members and their constituents of the undemocratic nature of the proposed reforms. The National Executive Committee immediately imposed a gagging order, and four Members were suspended from the European Parliamentary Labour Party because they would not sign such an order.

During this argument, and the parallel argument about restrictions on welfare, two Members were expelled. They have sought to consult within and outside the Labour Party on the need to establish an Independent Labour Network, ensuring a political space for the left, continuing the development of a relevant socialism encouraging and promoting new ideas, and defending and campaigning for:

- the defence and improvement of the welfare state, encompassing those reforms which can make it more responsive to the needs of its users, and more congenial and considerate to the people who work for it, whilst improving funding in a considerable number of neglected areas. Standards in Britain should be raised to equal the best in Europe;
- the introduction of strong measures for the redistribution of income, and the restoration of full employment across Europe as the basis for economic life;

- the inauguration of genuine reforms to de-centralise power to the localities, and bring those powers presently controlled by quangos back under democratic accountability, and the elimination of the democratic deficit at every level: European, national, regional and local;
- a return to policies designed to promote peace and nuclear disarmament.

The Independent Labour Network, however, does not seek to become another political party. It seeks to promote association between those who have supported the traditional social programme of the Labour Party, and to help organise protests against the ill-effects of New Labour's attacks on those policies. This has become necessary because the new rules and structure of New Labour, pushed through in the 1997 post-election honeymoon, prevent Labour members and Constituency Parties having any substantial control of, or even influence over, New Labour policy. This disenfranchises not only members but, more importantly, all those non-members, thinking people who lack wealth and power. No Party now speaks for them.

The Independent Labour Network seeks to ensure that there will be a political party speaking for ordinary people. Its preferred means of achieving this is by exerting sufficient pressure, internal and external, to persuade the Labour Party to return to this role. Only if this proved impossible would it be necessary to consider beginning again, to form a new Party of Labour. The historical Labour Party served three overlapping functions. It was the keeper of a social conscience. It was an agency for the defence and improvement of working and living conditions of all that part of the population which suffered most from inequality and discrimination. It was also an electoral machine, seeking to extend its representation in democratic assemblies in order to advance the other two functions.

Pluralism actually assisted these processes. It ensured that the social conscience could develop continuously, refining the approach to equality, and developing ideas of common ownership and democratic accountability. Pluralism served the pursuit of immediate objectives, and widened the electoral appeal of the Party as a whole.

New Labour has a minimal social conscience, ringed around and cramped by the constraints of the market place. The same constraints inhibit practical action to improve the condition of the poor, the low paid and the excluded. Up to now, however, New Labour has been successful in elections, in spite of these impediments. True, the 1997 election majority was smaller than that in the European elections of 1994, under John Smith's inspiration, but since then New Labour has won votes from many of the same people whose standards of life it has seemed determined to attack. How long can this continue?

The Independent Labour Network is consulting actively about the feasibility of protests in the electoral field. But it would be a profound mistake to concentrate only on this area, leaving a great vacuum where the conscience of the Labour movement used to exist, and lapsing back to live within the minimal space of individual compassion, where the necessary collective action in defence of decent standards of life has been subverted by managed conformity. There are other problems, of peace and environmental sustainability and public transport, to take three examples, which are being grossly mismanaged.

That is why we are launching the May Day Manifesto. The first part of this Manifesto concerns the maintenance of the Welfare State, and contests the reasoning of those who would seek to dismantle it. Other parts of a rolling manifesto will follow during the coming year. The reason we began at this point was quite simple: it was here that many of the most vulnerable people in society were coming under attack. Strong complaints by Labour and former Labour supporters have mitigated part of this cruel offensive. Some U-turns have been made. No doubt the focus groups which advise the Government on its growing unpopularity have made some contribution to tactical adjustments. But only open protests seem to have changed Government minds. Even so, disabled people have a great deal to fear from the continuance of the Benefit Integrity Project, which follows the precise strategy of its Conservative progenitors, in cutting, piecemeal, the cost of maintaining disabled people. Official rhetoric needs careful scrutiny where such matters are concerned, here, as in the promises now being made to the coal miners.

But this publication seeks to discern the wider picture as well as to assist the present victims of official cuts. To establish this wider analysis it is necessary to invite discussion, not only about the details of the argument, but also about its implications for future action. In this sense, we hope that the May Day Manifesto will provoke a continuing discussion, extending itself into other crucial areas of policy, and inviting responses from all those who used to expect from the Labour Party the intellectual space in which to develop ideas and ideals.

Today, New Labour has closed down this space, and it needs to be reopened. We have earlier made our protest about the Government's failure to maintain free higher education or to find money for its promised life-long learning project. We invite further contributions to the May Day Manifesto series, combining analysis and prescription. We shall seek to promote seminars and conferences which can assist this process, and help bring together the different streams of argument which develop. By May Day 1999, we hope to be nearer to a synthesis, which can help those inside and outside the Labour Party to clarify their objectives, and to resist the displacement of socialist values from the political argument.

The subversion of the Labour Party by New Labour Aliens may or may not be reversible. Control of a powerful machinery of patronage is a substantial asset for reaction, and there appears to be no shortage of generous contributions from powerful tycoons to ensure that the left remains permanently dispossessed of its traditionally political framework.

But socialist ideals will live, as long as socialists have the courage to tell the truth as they see it. This May Day Manifesto is an invitation to participate in an intellectual adventure: but it is also a challenge to the power of Mammon in the Labour movement.

THE UK STATE WELFARE BENEFIT SYSTEM, 1998/99
all figure are £s per week

Benefit	Single Person	Couple + 2 children	Single + 2 children	Notes
Job Seekers' Allowance Contributory: 50 x lower earnings limit (LEL) needed				
18-24	39.85	see Income Support below		means tested
25+ -60/65	50.35	ditto	ditto	after 6 months
LEL	64.00			

Other Non-means-tested benefits				
Sick Pay	57.70	see Income Support below		if earn min. £64; after 4 days; for 22 weeks
Incapacity – over 35 & under 60/65 yrs				
– first 28 weeks	48.80	+ 75.85	+ 51.90	extra for
– weeks 29-52	51.70	+ 66.95	+ 43.00	starting
– weeks 53+	64.70	+ 90.55	+ 52.75	before 35-44
Incapacity – 60/65 yrs				
– first 52 weeks	59.90	+ 57.00	+ 21.10	
Disability	38.70	Income Suport see below		if no NI
+ age additions				contributions
Disability Living or Attendance Allowance				
– lowest rate	13.60	Income Support see below		
– highest rate	51.30			
Industrial Disablement				
– 100%	104.70	Income Support see below		
– 40% etc.	41.88 etc.			
Constant Attendance Allowance				
– part-time	21.00			
– maximum	84.00			
Maternity Benefit				
– first six weeks 90% of pay		Income Support see below		Qualification: 41 weeks contribs before birthday at £64 p.w.
– 12-18 weeks	57.70			
Child Benefit				lone parent
– first child	. .	11.45	17.10	premium
– other children		9.30	17.10	ending June 1998 for new claimants
Widow's pension				
– husbands death				
over 55	64.70	Income Support see below		
over 45	19.41-60.17			
Basic Pension				
– standard rate	64.70	Income Suport see below		Qualification:
– wife	38.70			39/44 annual
– over 80	0.25			contributions
SERPS – average	+ 9.00			

Benefit	Single Person	Couple + 2 children	Single + 2 children	Notes
Means-tested Benefits				
Income Support				disregards: can
– under 18	30.30			earn up to £15;
– 18-24	39.85	124.65	100.70	savings up to £3000
– 25+	50.35	124.65	100.70	
elderly premiums				
– 60-74	20.10	couple 30.35		
– 75-79	22.35	couple 33.55		
– over 80 or over 60 disabled	27.20	couple 38.90		
disabled premiums				
– single	21.45	couple 30.60		
– severely disabled	38.50	couple 77.00		
– disabled child	21.45			
– carer	13.65			

Housing benefit
– available at full cost of rent etc., for those on Income Support, if net income is no more than personal allowance plus premium (e.g. pensioner couple £79.00 plus £30.35) and, if more, the benefit is reduced by the difference; income of non-dependents in the household will reduce the benefit available. This tapering is part of the poverty trap.

Council tax benefit
– available 100% for those on Income Support subject to deductions as incomes rise and for income of non-dependents in the household. Another poverty trap.

	Single Person	Couple + 2 children	Single + 2 children	Notes
– Family Credit				qualifying: in full
– over 16 hours	..	71.70	71.70	for those working
– over 30 hours	..	82.25	82.25	with income below £77.15 pw. and savings up to £3,000
Disability Working Allowances				
– over 16 hours or in proportion	49.55	101.65	101.65	only those earning less

Average Wages
– full time male manual 317.00
– part-time female non-manual 60.00-100.00

Modest-but-adequate Living Standard			
including car	177.44	368.41	348.08
+ income tax/NIC	49.76	96.00	113.07
- child benefit	00.00	20.35	26.10

Sources: Benefits from Labour Research Department, *State Benefits.*
Average earnings from Labour Research Department, *Fact Service*, vol.60, issue 3, 22nd January 1998
Living standards from the Family Budget Unit, Kings College London, quoted in Labour Research Department, *Fact Service*, vol.59 issue 50, 18 December, 1997

CHAPTER 1

Introduction and Summary

This Manifesto raises questions both of the practicalities and the philosophy of New Labour's proposals for reforming the British system of welfare. Eighteen years of Conservative Government began a process of dismantling the welfare state which long years of popular struggle, culminating in the enactments of post-war Labour governments, had established. When men and women were expropriated from the land which gave them a living, and they became dependent for their livelihood on the sale of their labour to an employer, they had to create a state which would guarantee their inalienable rights – to 'the preservation of life, liberty and the pursuit of happiness'.

The welfare state enshrined the fundamental belief in the equal creation of human beings to which they owe those rights. Any act which reduces those rights, which denies the equality of human creation and has the effect of dividing or excluding some sections of humanity by forms of apartheid, must on this basis be anathema. This does not imply a levelling down but a levelling up. It is not a matter of charity, although it does not exclude the motivation of generosity. It is not a matter of protection, although it does not exclude care for those who are disadvantaged mentally or physically. It is a recognition of human rights. In much of Europe, it is spoken of as solidarity or social cohesion; in Britain we call it welfare, the welfare of the whole community, a social guarantee of security. It had one weakness, a symptom of the times of its foundation; it treated the wage earning man and dependent wife as the norm.

The Conservative Inheritance
What Conservative Governments (and some Labour Governments)

17

have done has not only reduced the value of welfare provision, it has debased its meaning. What was designed by William Beveridge as a universal system of social insurance against sickness, unemployment, maternity, disability, widowhood and old age, to which all contributed while they could and from which all could draw when they were in need, has been steadily changed into a system of benefits granted to claimants. Special allowances for the task of rearing children, grants for child bearing, sick pay, unemployment assistance and the old age pension have all become state benefits, in the process perverting the original meaning of the Victorian 'benefit clubs' of mutual insurance. Our commonalty has been divided into those who are taxpayers and those who are claimants upon them.

To support the founding of the welfare state, a progressive taxation system was introduced, designed to require the rich to pay not just a larger share in relation to their wealth but a larger proportion of their income than those less well to do. What was said on the continent to be a solidarity tax was called in the UK 'redistributive' and was argued for not so much on moral grounds as on Keynesian economic grounds – for sustaining consumers' purchasing power as new capital investment increased the production of goods. Corporation taxes were also strengthened, and at one time an excess profits tax introduced, so that employers should contribute to maintaining the education and health of their workforces and the infrastructural services on which all their activities depend.

Mrs Thatcher's Governments ended the higher income tax bands and increased indirect taxes, which fall most heavily in proportion to their income on the poor. Her governments pursued a deliberate policy of creating unemployment – a worthwhile price to bring down inflation, as one of her Chancellors presumed. At the same time, successive Conservative governments, faced by rising expenditure on maintaining the unemployed, began to cut the value of state provision, particularly by ending in 1980 the link between pensions and earnings. The result of this was to reduce the pension from 21 per cent of average earnings to 14 per cent. At the present rate of decline, it would be half that in another 20 years. Despite the rise in the number of unemployed and the cost of supporting their incomes, the share of state expenditure in the national income has been reduced. It is now almost the lowest of any European government and the proportion of national income taken by taxes and national insurance contributions is absolutely the lowest.

As a result of these policies, British society has been ravaged by social violence against the poor which has corroded relationships, neighbourhoods and general well being. Social security provision in the UK has dropped from being one of the highest in Europe in relation to national income to being one of the lowest. The inadequacy of social insurance has forced more and more people onto social security (i.e. non-contributory benefits). Means testing has been applied to more benefits, rising from 16 per cent of welfare spending in 1979/80 to 37 per cent today, the highest proportion in any European country. At the same time, while the share of state spending devoted to income support has risen, employers' contributions have fallen, so that today they pay the lowest indirect costs for their labour – i.e. towards social security and vocational training. On overall labour costs, only employers in Spain, Greece and Portugal in the European Union have lower costs; while conditions of work and environmental effects are among the least regulated in the UK. When Mr Blair offered the British example of deregulation to the the rest of Europe, the President of the European Commission said that he hoped that there would be no competition for the prize of the 'sweatshop of Europe'.

What is New Labour Doing?

When a New Labour Government was elected in May of 1997, it was widely believed that Tony Blair's messianic zeal would be applied to staunching the wounds in the body politic, and reversing the eighteen years of decline in spending on welfare. The rhetoric of 'traditional Labour values' and support for communities, for giving unemployed men and women a hand up to work in place of a 'hand-out' on the dole, for enabling lone mothers and the disabled to afford child care and to receive assistance in finding work – all sounded most encouraging, despite the offensive language of charity. There was a snag – that Tory spending cuts were to stay in place for two years and only the £3.5 billion from the windfall tax on privatised utilities was to be available at once for moving the young and the long term unemployed 'from welfare into work'. There were nearly three million who said that they were ready to start work, if they could find it, and £3.5 billion, even allowing for reduced welfare spending and increased tax receipts, would only create jobs for 400,000. But this would be a start and promised help with the cost of child care could give many more women the opportunity to get out to work, and more could perhaps be expected later.

So it seemed, until the shock of the cut in the lone parent child benefit premium proposed by the Tories was not rescinded by Labour, and the changes made by the Tories in 1995 in relation to incapacity benefit were not reversed. Then in January 1998 in *The Times* newspaper Mr Blair announced a radical reform of welfare provision and set off to tour the country to argue for it. In support of this campaign, the Department of Social Security issued a series of 'Welfare Reform Focus Files'. These provided the so-called 'evidence' for Mr Blair's claim that the cost of welfare was becoming excessive and its provisions were not meeting the needs of the poorest people in the country. One of the reasons was the failure of many old people to make a claim for means-tested benefits when their state pension proved insufficient for their needs. Making a claim, which involves bureaucratic and insensitive procedures, was not the same thing as exercising the right to provision to which they had made their contributions.

This Manifesto takes up Mr Blair's argument and examines the supporting Welfare Reform Focus files, so as to compare the situation of Britain's welfare state today with what it was in the past and with welfare provisions made on the continent. It reveals the increasing inequality between rich and poor in Britain, which is more extreme now than in any other country in the European Union, and the resultant decline of Britain's position in all the indicators of relative human development. Low wages have combined with means tested benefits and regressive taxation to trap millions of men and women in poverty. On one count after another Britain is shown to be at the bottom of the pile in social protection relative to other European countries. This is the reality of the situation in which Mr Blair proposes that welfare spending in Britain is too heavy and savings must be made, with more provision targeted on the very poor (in other words, means-tested), and Mr Brown proposes, after a delay, to help those with children at the expense of those without.

Is this, then, the total effect of Mr Brown's budget? Undoubtedly, more money is to be made available in 1999 for child benefit and, in two year's time, for child care, but not new money – rather a switch from the single persons and childless couples, including the elderly and the widows, to the families with children. The aim here as in the schemes for 'welfare into work' is to make people more 'employable'. Mr Brown has promised in his new budget to guarantee that no one is to be worse off by going to work and that families where someone works full time will receive a minimum £180 a week, and their earnings of less than £220 a week will not be taxed.

Unanswered Questions

But this leaves many questions unanswered. What is £180 or £220 a week? The modern Rowntree estimate for a decent living for a couple or a lone parent with two children under 11 is twice these amounts. Where are the jobs to come from on which people can be employed? There are at least 1.5 million men and women chasing half a million job vacancies and great areas in the country where industries have been closed down and there simply are no jobs. The bribe for employers of £60 a week for taking on the young unemployed and £75 a week for the long term unemployed must mean that these new workers replace existing workers who do not have the subsidy attached to them. Is child benefit to be taxed? Will increased child benefit simply continue to reduce income support for women who cannot work? What does the earnings guarantee mean for working part-time, which is what most women with children prefer, but which carries no contributory insurance requirement from the employer and a wage too low to contribute from for private insurance? Will the contribution from the state to the costs of child care be enough, and paid promptly enough, to encourage women to look for work? And what happems to all the poor families and their children between now and the year 2000, when most of the new provisions come into force?

To seek to answer these questions, this Manifesto, therefore, begins with a careful examination of the Government's Green Paper and of the tax changes which Mr Brown is proposing to support the welfare 'reforms' of Mr Blair. The emphasis on shifting from welfare to work would be admirable if new jobs were being created to employ the young people, the lone mothers and the long term unemployed. Without that, increased incentives to find work are a bitter delusion. The moves towards individual pension rights for women would be excellent if they were not combined with privatising pension provision. For, this is both costly in administration and subject to gross mis-selling and even (as in the Maxwell pension funds) to fraud, and fails to build in any element of redistribution from rich to poor. Indeed, it exaggerates inequalities by leaving it to each individual to save for old age, with just a means-tested safety net for those who have no savings.

It is ominous that there is no mention in Mr Brown's budget speech of pensioners, despite the fact that they are a major recipient of state incomes including income support. The cuts in National Insurance contributions announced by Mr Brown must imply a further phasing out of the state pension and its replacement by occupational and private schemes. Employers in Britain, who already pay the least tax and social security contributions of any European country, are to pay still less, and the private insurance companies, whose high costs and mis-selling practices are a national disgrace, are to be the gainers. Is the next step to be privatising provision for unemployment, sickness and disability? Rather than reversing the Tories' dismantling of the welfare state, the silence on the state pension and the integration of National Insurance contributions with taxation suggests that this Government proposes to continue the process. Those who are young enough and can find work will benefit from the working families credits in the tax system, but for the old, the disabled and the childless poor there is little or nothing, not yet even a minimum wage.

What Could be Done?

The Manifesto ends with some proposals for reforms which would check the slide into poverty and re-establish the equality of citizen rights for which Labour has always fought in the past. They comprise chiefly the reinstatement of the higher income tax bands and the earnings link for pensions, together with the extension of the National Insurance Contribution upper limit and the ending of tax reliefs and of tax avoidance opportunities for the rich, so that the principle of universal social insurance can be re-established with a proper contribution from employers and from better-off tax payers with equal rights for women built in. Then Britain could have once again one of the more equitable, rather than the least equitable, of the welfare systems in Europe, but brought up to date by providing for the right of women to full separate treatment and encouraging individual supplementation of basic universal provision.

The proposals in this Manifesto, however, go beyond the essential task of reparation of past devastation and attempt to tackle the truly new challenge which the Twenty-First Century will reveal. This is not just that it should be possible for all men and women to be able to find rewarding work. Mr Blair and Mr Brown, in their emphasis on releasing people for work, are seeking to establish the work ethic of the past, not of the future. Most production, distribution and exchange in the past was labour-intensive. Today, machines increasingly replace the demand for labour. The challenge is to re-envisage what is work – in the home, in protecting the environment, in service to the community, in provision for recreational activities, in artistic expression, as well as in factories and transport, shops and offices. The challenge is to redistribute work, so that those who now work excessively long hours in offices and factories and other workplaces, generally under some form of compulsion, can be freed for pursuing wider interests, while others who now have little or no work outside the home can be included in the totality of social production and social life.

Far from realising the forward-looking image they seek to present, Messrs Blair, Brown and Field and the rest appear to be trying to revive the Victorian age of the bourgeois work ethic. Although Frank Field certainly looks the part, Mr Gradgrind and Samuel Smiles would seem unlikely prototypes for leaders of New Labour taking a New Britain into the new century. But that is what they are: the one demanding discipline and devotion to work from the young, the other encouraging individual self-improvement and self-reliance throughout life. These are not harmful objectives in themselves; everything depends on the goals within which they are set. In the perspective of Mr Blair and Mr Brown they are set within a goal of national competitiveness in the global economy that is hopelessly misplaced. The UK is not a large enough economy on its own to compete but needs joint and common action in Europe and more widely; and a competitive ethos is no longer a guarantee of success in a world of teams and networks. A new manifesto for Labour must set new goals for cooperative endeavour as well as for individual excellence. But that implies a framework of government which is designed to reduce inequalities, not to endorse them.

CHAPTER 2

The Green Paper

The Green Paper on the reform of welfare was presented to the House of Commons by Frank Field on March 26th as one further step in the revelation of the Government's true aims in refashioning the welfare state.

The Dance of Salome

Such disvestment is like the dance of Salome, in which New Labour reveals the naked truth about its intentions. As each garment from Labour's past is cast off, the initial shock is reduced, but anticipation of the final denouement aroused. No one quite expected that lone parents would lose their premium benefit or that the Tory assault on the disabled would be continued. Expressions of outrage and wholesale revolt at the spectacle were met with a clear statement from the highest authority that there was more to come. The Prime Minister himself launched a radical critique of the whole overdressed model that needed to be cut back. The cost and complexity of the outfit were, he said, intolerable – old fashioned and covering up fraud and abuse. The DSS released a description layer by layer of the entire wardrobe which weighed down upon the body politic. Titivating suggestions then appeared in the press of the next revelation: the Chancellor himself would provide work for the lady as she undressed. The budget was presented; there would be no more money except for work, and less clobber to carry around.

We are not yet at the final denouement with Frank Field. His mistress rushes onto the stage to hold the last veil of gauze across the vital parts, but the underlying shape is becoming clear. As the seven veils are cast aside, a fashionably thin, almost anorexic figure is revealed, but whose head will Salome demand, the young or the old, as she stands there shorn of all protective padding against winter's cold, homeless, penniless, alone – but free, free from state interference, free from smothering vestments, free to work for an employer, free to compete in the great world market, free to engage in a new contract with government.

We can abandon our metaphor now. For the title of Mr Field's Green Paper tells us all, the first half the spin; the second half the reality: *New Ambitions for our Country: A New Contract for Welfare.*

The New Social Contract – a Third Way?

The suggestion of a contract should not be misunderstood. Contracts, as every lawyer knows, are only required where the parties do not trust each other. Rousseau knew that. The social contract, to which Mr Blair appeals in introducing the Green Paper, is based upon the assumption of a mythical 'general will', by which the people are supposed to have delegated authority to the government. No doubt Mr Blair believes that the 43 per cent of the voters, 33 per cent of the electorate, in the UK, who voted for him represented that general will. Not for the first time. Rousseau's authority has been used to justify every kind of totalitarian government – fascist, communist and social democrat alike.

The 'blind multitude' needs to be guided, said Rousseau. 'Whoever refuses to obey the general will shall be compelled to do so by the whole body. This means nothing less than that [s]he will be forced to be free.' The 'tyranny of majorities' is as real a danger as that of minorities. Positive freedoms – the 'freedom to' - are at the heart of democracy, but the decisions of majorities have to be given what Alexander d'Entreves (in *The Notion of the State*) called 'a purely pragmatic value', remembering, as the saying goes, that counting heads is easier, and better, than breaking them or cutting them off. The right to 'have a say', particulalrly in matters that closely affect everyone, is a basic right, to be maintained whatever the problems it generates.

The philosophical foundations of Mr Blair's reforms, however, lie further back than Rousseau – in the justification that John Locke gave for men surrendering their freedoms to the state in a 'social compact' for 'the preservation of their lives, liberties and estates', the three basic goods that he sums up in one 'general name, property'. This was the philosophy of the emerging capitalist class, in the Seventeenth Century, rejecting the sovereignty of the monarch, and seeking maximum freedom from state interference for their ventures. It enshrines the concept of negative liberty – freedom from, not freedom to. The individual is sacrosanct and the state required only to defend those individual freedoms and to encourage the individual virtues of hard work self-reliance, self-improvement, self-advancement, such as Dickens depicted in Mr Gradgrind, and Samuel Smiles in his evocation of *Self Help*.

This political liberalism is closely associated with economic liberalism. Freedom for the individual means also freedom for the owner of capital, freedom for the employer, within limits set only by the effect on other employers. It supposedly leaves to the impersonal forces of the market the allocation of resources and the distribution of incomes. But in the market some, and especially those with capital, are more equal than others. Such liberalism stands at the opposite pole to socialism. To rectify inequalities which the market multiplies and to achieve anything approaching 'social justice' requires the intervention of the state. Competing individuals cannot assure anything except continuing and worsening inequalities. Forms of collective action are needed.

So, when Mr Blair in his introduction to the Green Paper proposes a 'third way' between privatisation and the *status quo* he says that he is looking towards 'a modern form of welfare that believes in empowerment not dependency'. But the empowerment is of the individual, not the collective. There is no suggestion of enhancing trade union power, very much the reverse. The individual needs to be free from restraints and controls, not only of the state but of others who would interfere in the market between capital and labour. The 'status quo' in welfare, to which Mr Blair refers, is what is left of socialist collective thinking after 18 years of Tory demolition.

Frank Field's Principles

This critique of the Green Paper is largely concerned with philosophy, and not with detailed proposals, because so is the paper iself. Advocates of assistance with child care for working mothers believe that their battle is largely won; what it will mean in detail when working mothers take in each other's children and share out the benefit is not clear. The disability rights movement also claims victory, in the retention of the disability living allowance as a non-means tested benefit and in the withdrawal of curbs on housing and council tax benefits. But this was reported by David Brindle in *The Guardian* (31.03.98) as being designed 'to clear the decks of anything that could upset the wider welfare reform programme'. The threat of stricter tests for new disability claimants remains, and Mr Field's hopes for state contributions to compulsory second tier pension schemes seem to have been firmly squashed by the Treasury.

So we can only look at the principles, of which the first is the 'New Welfare Contract'. *The Guardian* of 27.03.98 presents this with a pretty picture of the Secretary of State and her Minister.

New Welfare Contract

Duty of Government:
- Provide people with the assistance they need to find work.
- Make work pay.
- Support those unable to work so that they can lead a life of dignity and security.
- Assist parents with the cost of raising their children.
- Regulate effectively so that people can be confident that private pensions and insurance products are secure.
- Relieve poverty in old age where savings are inadequate.
- Devise a system that is transparent and open and gets money to those in need.

Duty of Individual:
- Seek training or work where able to do so.
- Take up the opportunity to be independent if able to do so.
- Give support, financial or otherwise, to their children and other family members.
- Save for retirement where possible.
- Not to defraud the taxpayer.

Duty of us all:
- To help all individuals and families to realise their full potential and live a dignified life, by promoting economic independence through work, by relieving poverty where it cannot be prevented and by building a strong and cohesive society where rights are matched by responsibilities.

Principle One: The Contract

Underpinning this contract lies the Government's commitment to encourage people to come off welfare and enter work – through the Welfare to Work and New Deal programmes, as well as through the changes announced in the budget to increase incentives. These will be considered later, but the key question is where the work is coming from. The programmes cited can easily mean no more than the replacement by employers of unsubsidised workers with subsidised ones. Incentives to escape the poverty trap and welfare dependence all assume that there are jobs to be found in the areas of high unemployment. There obviously aren't; and the young men who move away to find work only too often leave behind lone parents dependent on the vagaries of the Child Support Agency.

Principle Two: Supplementing the State Pension

The public and private sectors should work in partnership to ensure that 'wherever possible, people are insured against foreseeable risks and make provision for their retirement'. This in effect means a two tier-system with the state pension for most as the second tier, and a safety net for those whose incomes are inadequate for them to make their own provision. In practice, it is expected that the Government will offer low cost 'stakeholder pensions' to replace poor value private schemes, but the question of compulsory contributions to 'top up' the basic state pension is still being 'seriously considered'. The contribution from the employer has not been mentioned.

The rejection of any renewal of the link between the growth of earnings and the annual rise in the state pension and the rejection equally of improvements to SERPS, based on higher employer contributions, are deeply regretted and heavily criticised by pensions experts like Professors Peter Townsend and Alan Walker. Their criticism is on the grounds that all private schemes are much more expensive to administer and lack any redistributive element from the rich to the poor. The core of the state system has been the contributory social insurance principle, whatever concessions are made on child care and disability, and it is the abandonment of this principle for its largest element, the old age pension, in favour of individualism and privatisation that is at the heart of the reforms.

Principle Three: High Quality Services

The welfare state is not limited to cash benefits. The Green Paper emphasises that it incorporates a range of services – including education, health, transport, housing and child care. The third principle is that these should all be of 'high quality'. Housing benefit is referred to as a problem, which has defeated successive governments, but no indication is given of how it could be solved, except that fraud must be reduced. There is nothing about cheaper housing.

The reason for including this 'principle' is that there is a strong relation between social secrity, education and health. The needs of the education and health services could, so it is believed, be met without increasing the total of government spending, by cutting expenditure on social security. Mr Blair frequently complains that social security is now taking more public money than education and health together. It often has in the past depending on the level of unemployment. The idea that these should be competing demands on public resources is particularly stupid, because all three services are mutually supportive, and weakness or failure in one causes trouble in one or both of the others. Good education depends on good health and vice versa. Low incomes due to unemployment result in poor health and poor educational capacity. If Mr Blair is worrying about economic competitiveness, it is not only trained and healthy workers that he needs, but workers with a sense of security and confidence in the future for themselves and their families and for society in general.

Principle Four: Support for the Disabled

The Green Paper states that disabled people 'should get the support they need to lead a fulfilling life with dignity'. We have already reported the belief of the Disability Rights groups that early fears of cuts in the benefit for incapacity and of terminating the living and attendance allowances have been put to rest. Doubts remain as to whether more stringent tests in the future for incapacity benefit will not be used to reduce the number of new claimants so as to cut the £8 billion bill. The idea would be to switch any savings to cover the costs of the living allowances, which have been guaranteed continuation on a non-means tested basis.

Much of the talk about fraud centres around claims for disability benefits. These have risen rapidly with rising unemployment. The change in the criteria for disability, from what the claimant cannot do to what he or she can do, may be very encouraging in one way, but it neglects consideration of the kind of jobs that are available in different areas. Where there is high unemployment, any disability is likely to make the finding and keeping of employment exceedingly precarious. The Disability Rights organisations are pleased that living and attendance allowances will remain a national and universal benefit, not means-tested or farmed out to local authorities. On the other hand, the various forms of support for disabled old people that are available from the social service departments of most local authorities are extremely valuable. Many have already been cut back by Tory government capping of local government spending and the threat to cut them back still further would involve a serious loss of amenity.

Principle Five: Support for Families and Children

This is supposedly covered by the provisions for child care tax credits for working mothers in Mr Brown's March budget. How this will work out is still unclear. Nothing will be available under this heading, except continuing child benefit payments, until 1999 and the details of the subsidies to be made have not been announced. But the question has already been raised about the possibility of two separate parents registering as child minders and taking in each others' children to claim the tax credit against their income from going out to work. More seriously the needs of parents who choose to stay at home and look after their young children have not been addressed. Forcing such women to go out to work cannot be a sensible idea.

Once more, as with the disabled, there will be a problem for women in areas of high unemployment of finding work, even if the child care costs are subsidised. Women with children are much less able than men to pull up their roots and move to another part of the country where jobs are less scarce. Mr Brown has tried to deal with the poverty trap that makes it uneconomic for people to go out to work when they lose more in benefit than they gain in income after they have paid taxes and National Insurance contributions. It is far from certain that Mr Brown's provisions will be adequate to overcome the traps that exist and there is much in the detail of tax credit systems that has still not been announced.

Principle Six: The Attack on Poverty and Social Exclusion

'Specific action' is proposed 'to attack social exclusion and help those in poverty.' Unlike the UN Development Programme, there is no aim to eliminate poverty, let alone to end social exclusion. The Green Paper proposes an integrated approach to preventing deprivation, and policies will be coordinated by the Social Exclusion Unit in Whitehall. This is surprising on two grounds: first, the causes of poverty and social exclusion tend to be local and to vary from place to place; second, the Social Exclusion Unit is headed up by Mr Mandelson, whose responsibility for the Millennium Dome would seem to be all consuming.

Poverty which affects one third of all children in the UK is a blight beyond all others. The causes of poverty will be examined later, but it is necessary to point out here that the main causes lie in low incomes and the tax system and not in the welfare system of benefits. Moreover, contrary to Mr Brown's indications, the largest proportion of those in the lowest income groups are already in work. Most of his measures for encouraging people to move from welfare into work do not apply. Much depends here on the level at which a minimum wage is set, when it comes to be introduced. But poverty is such a multifaceted problem that a single element like a minimum wage will not solve it. The question is whether there is the political will to eliminate and not simply to alleviate poverty in all its aspects.

Principle Seven: The Assault on Fraud

The aim that is stated that the reforms should be such as 'encourage openness and honesty' can only be commended. The emphasis that is placed upon the issue of fraud is, however, part of the spin doctoring designed to prepare public opinion for accepting the need to reduce social security expenditure. The actual evidence of fraud is slight and the figures of £3 billion to £4 billion of losses are simply wild guesses. Several comprehensive inquiries have concluded that the problem is not a serious one. Baroness Hollis, who heads up the Benefits Integrity Project, stated in January that they had yet to find a case of fraud.

The issue of benefit fraud is discussed later. What is quite evident is that the threat of withdrawal of benefits, especially from those with disabilities, has caused enormous distress. The organisation *Disability Rights Now* in a submission to the Secretary of State has published a number of harrowing case studies, and they seem to have had some effect, resulting in something like a 'U' turn by the Government on its most damaging proposals. It remains quite extraordinarily offensive to those who are suffering from some disabling condition that Ministers persist in assuring the public that people in 'genuine need' have nothing to fear. We will all know of someone who is in worse plight than we are and hesitate before asking for support, but if we have paid our contributions throughout our working lives, we should feel able to claim of right and not from charity. The number who do not claim benefits to which they are entitled is officially recognised to be far greater than any number who claim falsely. It is widely agreed, moreover, among those who have studied the problem that losses from tax avoidance and tax evasion are infinitely greater than any from benefit fraud. It is just that individual cases are less likely to be reported in the tabloid press, unless the case involves a Government minister.

Principle Eight: Better Delivery

The Green Paper regards the matter of what it calls the 'delivery of the service' as in need of 'modernisation' to 'improve customer satisfaction', so that customers can regard the system as personalised and tailored to their needs. All those who are in receipt of means-tested benefits and those which depend on medical or other professional opinion would probably agree, but the language employed tells us much about the cast of mind of the new Government. The population is treated as customers seeking satisfaction, not citizens exercising their rights. This is even out of keeping with the Paper's concept of a contract involving rights and obligations. Customers are not usually seen as having obligations except not to steal, to pay promptly and to queue in an orderly fashion. It follows only too closely the trend of the Government's thinking about welfare reform – that welfare is about benefits, more or less graciously, supplied by the tax payer to those who cannot look after themselves.

This is profoundly offensive not only to any socialist but to anyone who regards the equal humanity of all men and women as an important principle, however little observed in practice. But the emphasis on self help has a serious implication for the costs of 'delivery'. It has been estimated that about 10 per cent of income would be needed for an adequate 'stakeholder' pension such as the Government is proposing to supplement the existing state pension. Much of the increased cost would be swallowed up by the charges of the private insurance companies – a figure of 25 per cent is generally assumed. What sort of modern, satisfactory delivery service is that, when the expense ratio of the National Insurance Fund is less than 3 per cent and falling? One Life Assurance Company is quoted by the National Pensioners' Convention as saying that 'SERPS presents enormous benefits in terms of absolute portability, extremely low costs and efficient distribution systems.' So why go private?

The 34 Targets

It is reported that no fewer than 38 drafts of the Green Paper were scrapped before the final publication appeared. This is perhaps not surprising. This Government has brought to a fine art the presentation of policies in such a way as to give the impression of a commitment to actions which on closer examination prove to have no substance. Not only has the Treasury to be satisfied that no more money will be spent, but the business community and indeed all of 'Middle England' have to be reassured that they won't be paying any more. It might seem a bold undertaking in the Paper for the Government to set 34 measures of success by which its progress should be judged 'over the next 10 to 20 years'. Mr Field claimed that this is the first time a Government has ever set itself measures by which it could be judged. But what are the measures?

The fact is that nearly all the targets are sufficiently lacking in detail of quantities and dates as to be largely meaningless. The tone was clearly set in the New Welfare Contract, in which it is said to be a 'Duty of us all' to 'relieve poverty where it cannot be prevented'. In Clare Short's Department for International Development White Paper, the target is set of *eliminating poverty* within two decades. Poverty elimination on a world scale is an infinitely larger and more intractable problem than anything that exists in the UK. But then there was no danger that the Treasury would be asked to underwrite the cost of the whole exercise.The only absolutely firm commitment in the list appears to be the setting up of a Disability Rights Commission, although even this does not have a time scale attached to it.

The most striking aspect of the targets set for itself by the Government is the large proportion that are concerned with getting more people into work. This is evidently the over-riding aim of

Government policy. Examples are

- a reduction in the proportion of working age people living in workless housholds;
- a reduction in the proportion out of work for more than two years;
- an increase in the number of working age people in work;
- an increase in the proportion of lone parents and the disabled who are 'in touch with the labour market';
- a reduction in the proportion of children in workless households;
- an increase in the proportion of parents meeting their financial obligations to their children;
- discrimination against the disabled in obtaining employment should be reduced so that there are more disabled in work;
- greater collaboration between Benefits Agency and Employment Service to promote jobs, not dependency.

Even though no figures for increases or reductions are given and no dates apart from the 10 to 20 years, this is a pretty high-risk set of targets. Given the Government's extreme reluctance to create jobs and total reliance on the market to find employment for those who are made 'employable', the chances of an increase in employment and even a reduction in unemployment must be slim. Increases in productivity in the supply of both goods and services mean more output with fewer workers. And there is no reason to suppose that Mr Brown's fiscal management can avoid the regular occurrence of recessions. Perhaps it is hoped that the Goverment will come to be judged in the next boom that follows the next slump.

On pensions, the targets are suitably vague: a 'guarantee of a decent income in retirement for all' and an increase in the amount of money going towards savings and insurance – though without increasing the proportion borne by government; more people having 'high quality second tier pensions'; and confidence in the regulation of the market increasing. What is a decent income, and how pensions should be related to earnings is not dealt with. Nor is there anything about reducing the proportion of private pension contributions going to the insurance companies' charges. Or is that included in the phrase 'high quality' used in reference to second tier pensions?

The usual pious sentiments are uttered about openness and honesty in the system and about clearer conditions for eligibility for benefit, and especially for disability benefits. But there is one fairly definite promise

– that a cut in spending on incapacity benefit (which is not means tested) is planned to release resources for the more severely disabled. Less should be lost, it is promised, through fraud and fewer incorrect payments should occur, but what are the figures now against which comparison might be made? Customer satisfactions with the benefit system should increase, but again what measures exist now for making comparisons? There should be an increase in public service ethos and more job satisfaction among welfare staff. This is an interesting exception to the general drive coming from the Government for more private agencies in national services and for more competitiveness internationally. In fact, it is a quite remarkable concession to the principle of public service, in place of private profit, and an important indication that competition is out of place in social service. So we read that there is to be less duplication between agencies and best use of new technology in effecting cooperation. Once again, one can commend, but one wants to know what are the bench marks.

On health and education there are a wide range of targets, some very general like 'improved health' measured by longer life and longer sickness-free life; and a better model for tackling problems in the most deprived neighbourhoods. Others are more specific, though without quantities or time scales: more 11 year olds with good literacy and numeracy skills, fewer school leavers without qualifications, fewer school expulsions, fewer teenage pregnancies; finally, fewer people sleeping rough. There is no reference to the UNDP Human Development Index and any of the UNDP's criteria. It would be a real success if the UK could get back on the index to third place among European countries which it held in 1960, or to the fifth held in 1980, from the tenth place to which it has fallen today.

Rhetoric and Reality
The Green Paper claims that its aim is to break the traditional welfare mould in three crucial respects:
– to move from simply paying benefits to enabling people to move into work;
– to move from dispensing cash to also providing services of information and advice;
– to move from merely alleviating poverty to ensuring that everyone can develop their talents to the full.

Harriet Harman writing in *The Guardian* (31.03.98) claims that 'we will redistribute', but 'not by high taxes and handouts to the poor' which are policies which she says have been rejected by the electorate. There is no mention, however, in the article of any other form of redistribution, except, and this is not unimportant, in power between men and women in getting access to work. She might argue that there was redistribution between single people and people with children in the budget, but she doesn't say so; and it might be said that the subsidy offered to employers under 'Welfare into Work' projects to take on young and long-term unemployed involves a redistribution of jobs from the currently employed to the currently unemployed, but she would not admit to that. If redistribution does not mean resources being moved from the rich to the poor, it has lost its normal meaning; but what Harriet Harman calls the electorate – that is the marginal voters in Middle England – have become convinced, almost certainly wrongly in the long term, that such would not be in their best interests.

The fact is that capital accumulation in a capitalist economy inevitably polarises wealth and poverty. If this is not offset by redistribution through government taxation, there will not be the purchasing power among the mass of consumers to buy the extra goods and services that steady increases in productivity make available. Production will have to be cut back and unemployment will spread from the periphery to the heart of Middle England. Fear and insecurity are already gaining ground, but the answer is not to cut back on government taxing and spending. Unless taxes are raised from the smaller number who are better off and reduced for the larger number who are less well off, inequalities cannot be rectified, welfare reform is a sham, fiddling little bits of money from here to there, poverty will persist and economic recession become inevitable.

The rest of this Manifesto will be concerned with putting together the whole jigsaw of government taxing and spending, and relating the government's role in the development of the economy. In doing this we shall have to look at what has been done to the British welfare system in the last 18 years of Conservative rule, how it now compares with welfare systems in the rest of Europe, why the Blair 'reforms' are based on a false analysis and what can now be done to rescue something from the ruins. The argument will not be for going back to where we were in 1979 or 1949 but for building on what was good in the old system to adapt it to new developments.

CHAPTER 3

What Mr Brown is Offering

On March 17th Gordon Brown presented his second budget. It had been preceded by a flurry of official spinnings about the radical reforms that it would contain. These would build the foundations of a new welfare state in Britain, which would reward work, while protecting those who could not work. The spinnings had become necessary because of the strength of the public reaction, including a full scale revolt of Labour members in the House of Commons, at Government proposals for reducing the benefit paid to lone parents and the tightening up of allowances for disablement. Both these measures had been proposed by the previous Tory administration, but it had not been supposed that Labour would proceed with them. When Mr Blair set off to tour the country to argue for the reform of the welfare state, fears grew that it was not reform but a total dismantling that was being planned.

The 1998 budget had then to be seen, not just as a report on the state of the British economy with the Chancellor's proposals for its future direction, together with the usual tax adjustments, but as an indication of the nature of the taxation and public spending system that New Labour was introducing. Mr Brown sought to establish his pre-eminence as both a prudent treasurer and a radical thinker. There would be no exceeding of the spending limits set by the previous government, except for the £3.5 billion windfall tax on privatised public utilities, but other monies would be targeted to ensure that they met real needs and encouraged all who were physically capable to seek employment. The radical measures were to be found in the combining of taxation and national insurance, the replacement of certain benefits by tax credits, and a switching of tax rates and allowances, plus a sweetener of an increase beyond the retail price rise to be introduced to the child benefit in 1999.

Bombers or Children?

In preparing his budget, no doubt Mr Brown had to make what Mr Blair likes to call 'hard choices' – between bombers and children, for example. For it so happened that, just as the Treasury was making a tough review of 'defence' expenditure – 'not a cost-cutting exercise', said Mr Robertson, 'but a re-examination of our defence requirements from first principles' – along came a requirement from President Clinton to support his threat of military action against Saddam Hussein. And 'first principles' include Mr Blair's promise of a 'strong defence capability as an essential part of Britain's foreign policy'. What, then, was to be cut, if expenditure was to be kept within the last government's budget total? Did the Treasury have a view on the arms build-up around Iraq, which is still in place, to maintain the threat to Saddam Hussein?

Replacing a single Tornado lost in war or military exercises costs over £50 million, and the new Eurofighters which the government has just ordered – 232 of them – will cost £69 million each. That is £16 billion for fighter-bombers to be delivered from the year 2002 – or three years of current Child Benefit payments for the 12.5 million children on benefit in Britain. Hard choices! But it seems that they have already been made and the children get nothing more in real terms until 1999 and 2000, except that the under 11 premium on income support and family credit is to be raised in November of this year. The increases are delayed because monies are not yet available for such public spending.

It is said that the Eurofighter order will keep 40,000 people at work, but how many jobs will be lost, if all the families with children lose £10 a week for the next two years and more after that, to bring the children's allowance back to its original value? It must be many more jobs that would follow because what is bought for children – food, housing and heating, clothes and shoes, child care, school books, holidays – involve much more labour-intensive production than aircraft. While the Tories cut back military spending, there was no peace dividend. Welfare was cut too. Indeed, it was cut to an extent that can only be described in Professor Ken Jones's words as 'the ravages of 18 years of devastation and social violence of Conservative social policy ... corroding relationships, neighbourhoods and general well being'. It is in response to this situation, which is very similar to that faced by the Labour Government in 1945 after the ravages of war and decades of social violence in the 1930s, that New Labour was expected to act. Mr

Brown's budget must be judged in that light.

But the Government is arguing that scarce tax-payers' money can be targeted more effectively at the poor in other ways than by universal provision. Even the child benefit is to be taxed. 'Targeting' is the new euphemism for means-testing; and child benefit is the old family allowance by another name, a new name that emphasises its nature as a benefaction to the so-called 'deserving poor', those in 'real need', and not the universal right of a free citizen, like the right to vote. The first step of changing the name, from an allowance to a 'credit', which was taken by the last Tory Government, paved the way for New Labour to end the universality of the provision. Mr Brown's budget, for the first time since the 1945 Labour Government accepted the Beveridge Report, distinguishes between a child benefit for the unemployed and a tax credit for children of the employed. Mr Brown says that he has not forgotten those in need, while granting dignity to those in work. What he seems to have forgotten is the cost of administering means-tested benefits. Targeting cannot be 'cost effective', if 15-20 per cent of the cost disappears in the administration of means testing, when it is only 1 per cent for universal benefits.

The Income and Poverty Traps

Mr Brown has made a great appeal to public opinion that he has come to the rescue of the children in poverty. His appeal is that their parents or single parent should go out to work and he has considered what it is that is stopping them. The first obstacle that he has identified is that they cannot afford child care. So, he is to make a tax allowance for part of the cost of child care provision at a registered centre. The second is the poverty trap and associated with it the income trap. They reinforce each other: the one results because benefits actually provide more income than a low paid job, and taper off as income from a job rises, the most importing being Family Credit, but including also Housing Benefit and Council Tax relief; the other results from rising tax and insurance contributions exceeding a rise in income. Both combine to discourage men and women from seeking work when the wages for available work are extremely low. Mr Blair has suggested that the choice of living on welfare, so-called 'hand-outs', has become a preferred way of life, implying that the high level of benefits creates a dependency culture.

The 'poverty trap' is well illustrated in the diagram and case study taken from the Borrie Report on Social Justice (see below). 'Family credit, according to the most recent figures, is not claimed by nearly two out of every five people who should benefit from it, at an average loss to them of £22.25 per week and a total under-payment of some £200 million. One-fifth of those entitled to Income Support do not claim it – more than a million people; amongst elderly people alone, it is estimated that 570,000 do not claim their Income Support. Means-tested benefits, which cannot prevent poverty, are also remarkably inefficient at relieving it.

Moreover, these benefits are extremely expensive to administer. For

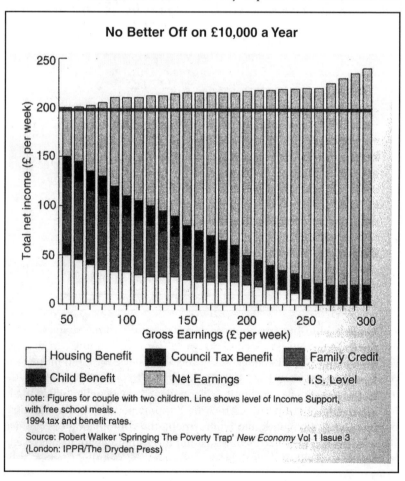

No Better Off on £10,000 a Year

note: Figures for couple with two children. Line shows level of Income Support, with free school meals.
1994 tax and benefit rates.

Source: Robert Walker 'Springing The Poverty Trap' *New Economy* Vol 1 Issue 3 (London: IPPR/The Dryden Press)

Trapped in Poverty

I am a married man with three sons and one daughter and I currently work for the Benefits Agency. The very poor salary offered causes me to have to claim state benefit in the form of Family Credit. The totally inescapable position I find myself in is that I am far, far worse off for going to work.

Working		*Income Support*	
£114.00	Take-home salary	£135.95	IS
£85.00	Family Credit	£34.30	Child Benefit
£34.30	Child Benefit		

£233.30		£170.25	

Less rent £35, council tax £11 approx, no school meals	No rent, no council tax, free school meals, clothing grant etc

£188 to manage on each week
for six people – ie food, clothes, gas,
electric, water etc.

So for less than £20 I am working and still feel a failure to my family. *Please* do not use my name, since I cannot risk upsetting my employers.

Letter to the Commission on Social Justice, April 1994

---

every £1 paid in Income Support, 11p is spent on administration, while every £1 paid from the Social Fund costs 45p to administer. In striking contrast, £1 in Child Benefit costs 2p to administer, and £1 in retirement pension only just over 1p.'

Means-testing also encourages dependence on benefits, rather than independence. Not only does Income Support penalise extra earnings, but as people move back into employment, the combination of National Insurance Contributions, income tax and the withdrawal of means-tested benefits means that half a million of the poorest people are effectively paying marginal tax rates of 70 per cent or even higher, creating a very long 'poverty plateau' where families can remain on low incomes for a very long time.

All the welfare benefits taper off sharply as income rises, except Child Benefit, leaving the new worker no better off, and indeed faced by National Insurance contributions and taxes to pay. In the Social Justice example, the poor man 'trapped in poverty' gave his wage as 'take-home salary'. He will probably have paid 3 per cent of gross wages as NIC and 20 per cent as tax. Mr Brown has done nothing to change the balance of direct and indirect taxation.

What is not always made clear is that the main reason for the poverty and income traps is not the high level of benefit but the low level of wages. These have been further reduced since the abolition of the Wages Councils and the Fair Wages Resolution of the House of Commons, and, until a minimum wage is introduced at a reasonable level, seem likely to remain low. Mr Brown places great emphasis on the results of the Welfare into Work projects, since these will both help the unemployed to prepare for work and to find it, but will also raise wages by a £60 subsidy for six months for employers taking on young unemployed people and £75 for long term unemployed. This is to be financed from the £3.5 billion windfall tax on the privatised utilities. £3.5 billions sounds like a lot of money, but not perhaps when compared with last year's estimated (National Institute *Economic Review*, 1/98, p.15) £36 billion windfall gains for those who had money to lend, from the conversions and de-mutualisations of building societies and life insurance companies. Recent calculations, moreover, indicate that it costs £9,000, net of tax gains and benefit savings, to create one new job. So, the £3.5 billions, if it were all spent on job creation, would create rather less than 400,000 jobs. Current numbers of unemployed on the claimant count amount to 1.5 million, but the Labour Force Survey reckons the true figure of workless to be nearly twice that number, or 10 per cent of the workforce, including half a million young people and an equal number of long term unemployed.

Of course, 400,000 new jobs would be a good start, if that is how the money is to be spent. Unfortunately, the utilities tax is a one-off and is not to be repeated and a subsidy to employers will keep wages low and encourage them to take on subsidised workers in place of their present unsubsidised ones. Employers will no doubt be required to promise not to do this and to retain their new workers after the six months' subsidy ends. But experience of 'workfare' in the United States, from which the idea was taken, suggests that it becomes a game of musical chairs, in which one worker in 10 still finds no place. It is also a fact that most of the poorest families are not poor because their members are unemployed, but because they are so poorly paid – in the income trap. Mr Brown has a plan for them too, to help those in work as well as those who reject the work alternative. This is the 'Working Families Tax Credit', another idea borrowed from the United States.

Working Families Tax Credit

The idea of a tax credit is that, in advance of a worker's annual tax return, an allowance is made by the Inland Revenue against the tax due; this in future will be made not only for a married couple and children, but also for low income and possibly for other considerations like child care costs and disability allowances. For the great majority of people the employer will simply allow for this in the calculation of Pay-As-You-Earn (PAYE). Only about a quarter of all taxpayers fill in a tax return. It is not certain whether the employers will be prepared to take on this responsibility without compensation.

The advantages of the scheme are that it is easy to understand and cheap to administer and doesn't appear to be a benefit and therefore seen as a hand out either by the recipient or the taxpayer. It seems to be in some ways like the old family allowance, which had been very popular with women. They could claim it themselves, without it depending on the partner's income, and they received it promptly for six months at a time. The disadvantages are that, unlike the family allowance, it has to be based on family and not on individual income and is normally paid to the man as chief income earner. Some critics have also complained that it puts undue pressure on mothers of young children to go out to work, when this may not be the best thing for the children.

Much has been made in the press of the fact that Mr Brown's new tax credit includes a subsidy for child care. When the Tax Credit was first mooted for introduction in the UK, there were complaints that it would offend the principle of separate taxation for women, since tax credit would be assessed on household income. Dawn Primarolo, the Treasury Minister involved, has assured women that they could fill in a box on the form of application, indicating that they wished to be paid direct and not through their partner's pay packet, through 'the purse and not the wallet', as the phrase goes.

The Institute for Fiscal Studies has commented that this concession spoils the whole purpose of the scheme, because it was designed to be applied automatically with the pay cheque, wherever rates of pay were below a certain level, thus avoiding the disincentive of form filling, the stigma of means testing, and of course the cost to the Inland Revenue of administration. It would, further, reduce the scale of benefit payments by excluding the better off mothers and appear to reduce it even more by calling the tax credit a tax break, and not a benefit.

In the event, the Government's scheme will, according to the Institute, be 'little different from family credit'. This is paid at present directly to about 725,000 women, treble the number since it was introduced in 1988. It replaced the old Family Income Supplement. Sixty per cent of the beneficiaries are either single parents or in families where the woman is the main wage earner. Reducing Child Benefit and increasing Family Credit not only involves more means testing – this has already risen from being applied to 17 per cent of all benefits in 1978/9 to being applied to 36 per cent in 1996 – but it implies well recognised uncertainties and delays in payment for the beneficiaries. Since only about a half of current Family Credit recipients were paying income tax when their award began, the Inland Revenue would find itself dealing with up to a third of a million extra assessments – at considerable extra cost.

Mr Brown has thought of that, and has excluded those earning below £220 per week from liability for income tax; and all 20 million employees will receive a cut in their National Insurance Contribution, so that no one pays for the first £81 of their weekly earnings. Whereas previously, according to Mr Brown, a family with two children paid tax even when they earned only 25 per cent of average earnings, in future there will be no income tax bill until they earn over 50 per cent of average earnings. Employers' contributions will also be reduced on low earnings – a further reason for employers' continuing to pay low rates, but part of the Government's desire to make Britain a cheap labour country.

Child Benefit and Low Wages

Is that what it is all about? The simple fact of the matter is that all these payments – Income Support and Family Credit – are designed to supplement wages which are so low that they are not enough to live on. They then have two untoward results. They discourage employers from paying higher wages and keep people and especially women in a state of what is called 'welfare dependency', either in low-paid work or in the poverty trap. The great majority of the poorest families are not the elderly, but those with children. Nearly one-third of all children in the UK live in households with an income that is defined as below the poverty line. That is the largest proportion of any country in the European Union and compares with France and Germany where only 12-13 per cent of children are in poverty. The original idea of a Family Allowance or Child Benefit was to ensure a guaranteed income for mothers of children as of right, and that is how it remains throughout most of Western Europe. Only Ireland has a similar proportion of means tested family benefit as the UK.

According to the TUC's statement on 'The Future of the Welfare State' in its 1998 Budget Priorities submission to the Chancellor,

'An interim report by the Social Security Committee, which has drawn together much of the evidence submitted by the Taylor Taskforce on the integration of tax and benefits, concludes that "for some commentators, the most effective targeting of resources towards families with children is Child Benefit" and that improvements to this one benefit could be the most straightforward way to improve the incentives of work for low income families. The TUC believes that the Government should pay close attention to widespread support for using Child Benefit as a pivotal measure in any long-term reform of the tax and benefits system to help make work financially attractive for low income families.'

While recommending the Chancellor to delay a major reform in the tax and benefit system until there has been more time for consultation, the TUC believed that the Government should

'immediately invest in measures which will provide financial assistance to poor families and the low paid by maximising the returns from engaging in employment. This would be achieved by using money from the reserve to finance a combination of measures: increasing Child Benefit rates to make work more financially attractive for poor families and by modifying the national insurance contribution rules in order to enable the very low paid to qualify for a range of contributory benefits that they are currently excluded from.'

No doubt the 'reserve' will by now have disappeared into the massive deployment of arms against Saddam Hussein. But the case for Child Benefit remains as a universal right and as an immediate requirement to alleviate poverty and not after a year's delay. The well-known expert on Social Policy, Professor Peter Townsend, in an open letter 'For the benefit of Tony Blair' (*Tribune*, 13.2.98) concurs with the TUC's judgement:

> 'The severity of the poverty trap will not be reduced by continuing to increase different forms of means-tests. By introducing more adequate benefits of right, including child benefit and pensions, means-tests and "perverse" incentives can be reduced. Tax and contribution rates among the rich can be adjusted to ensure both "fair" and comprehensive benefit coverage.'

Means Tests or Social Insurance

This is the heart of the matter – means testing or higher tax and contribution rates? Professor Townsend insists that

> 'Welfare Reform can be achieved by using well-tried, successful and popular institutions [he specifies contributory insurance and progressive tax and contribution rates] and not by going down an ill-conceived and mistaken course involving an excessive and entirely untried role for privatisation and means testing along with further cuts in public spending. If pursued this course of action will make matters worse, by enlarging both poverty and social polarisation.'

Where Working Families Tax Credits have been applied in Canada, a Social Security specialist in Toronto is quoted by the *Financial Times* (13.2.98), writing of a report by Professor John Hills which was commissioned by the Joseph Rowntree Foundation, that

> 'it proved expensive, poorly targeted and ineffective as a work incentive ... most recipients would have worked without it, while it produced high marginal tax rates for recipients as the money was withdrawn.'

Canada has decided to replace it and is considering a higher level of universal Child Benefit, equal to Income Support paid to those out of work, and to meet the extra cost, separate child payments in Income Support and the Married Couple's tax allowance and Family Credit could be dispensed with, and high income families would be more heavily taxed.

That would really be something for Mr Brown to think about. In the meantime, Professor Townsend warns him that 'tax credits are a mirage and a distraction, as the Conservative Government of the early '70s discovered'. And, if any cynics should query Townsend's belief in the popularity of the 'well-tried and successful institutions', let them try polling those who have made life-long National Insurance Contributions with a question about Frank Dobson's kite flying – that 'ministers must consider means testing the basic state pension' – a quite superfluous try-on, because opinion polls have revealed that a great majority of the people would pay more taxes anyway to help Mr Dobson to preserve the National Health Service (NHS).

So what is the problem about universal social insurance as the basis for a welfare state and about increasing pension payments and Child Benefit? Mr Blair says that it all costs too much and doesn't reach the right people. 'Middle England', it is said, does not approve of 'hand-outs' which are not targeted at the deserving poor. If that is true, 'Middle England' is making a big mistake, because they are major beneficiaries; and, if he really wants more of the poor to take up the benefits to which they are entitled, Mr Blair should recognise that they all take up the universal state pension as of right, but hesitate to go through all the hassle and suffer the stigma of claiming a supplement. Mr Blair has set out to teach them, anyway, what is good for them. The answer from both him and Mr Brown is that they must all go out to work – men and women, married and unmarried, with and without children, old and young, fit and disabled – and earn enough to save up for their old age, and possibly for other eventualities like sickness and unemployment. Going on in the old way just could not be afforded. It was all costing too much, they say. But the fact is that many will not be able to save enough and need support by right and not as a concession. Government spending in the UK is the lowest as a proportion of national income of any country in the European Union, barring only Ireland and Luxemburg.

Let me repeat that with emphasis.

Public expenditure in the UK is the lowest in proportion to national income of any country in the European Union, barring only Ireland and Luxemburg.

And, just in case you hadn't got it, in capital letters:

PUBLIC EXPENDITURE IN THE UK IS THE LOWEST IN PROPORTION TO NATIONAL INCOME OF ANY COUNTRY IN THE EUROPEAN UNION, BARRING ONLY IRELAND AND LUXEMBURG.

1998

BLAIR VERBIAGE

...STEM THAT..... TACKLES POVERTY." — TONY BLAIR, 15·1·98·

CHAPTER 4

Starting from Beveridge

Mr Blair's belief that the welfare state costs too much and requires a 'Big Bang', led him to launch a great campaign for its reform early in 1998, even in advance of Gordon Brown's budget and the publication of a Green or White Paper. Carefully placed leaks to friendly journalists were designed to test out responses to particular proposals and to prepare public opinion for what was to come. The main evidence for the supposed need for reform was contained in a Department of Social Security statement, comprising seven 'Focus Files' on *The Case for Welfare Reform*. It was announced that this was to be followed by a Green Paper, setting out a 'framework for policy' and finally a White Paper proposing legislation. This process is supposed to educate the public, but it would be better described as brain washing, as there is no discussion of alternatives.

The Beveridge Principles
The DSS statement starts from Beveridge. One would asume from a civil service document that it would be objective, at least in its statement of fact. But it begins with a so-called summary of 'Beveridge's Principles', which, it is said, 'will remain central'; and the fact is that the central principle of the Beveridge Report is omitted. This was that the welfare system should be 'comprehensive and universal'. Instead, *The Case for Welfare Reform* states only the following supposed 'Beveridge Principles':

'1. Society has a responsibility to help people in genuine need, who are unable to look after themselves;

2. Individuals have a responsibility to help provide for themselves when they can do so;

3. Work is the best route out of poverty for people who are able to work;
In addition fraud and abuse should be minimised and rooted out wherever found.'
A careful scouring of Beveridge's 1942 Report on *Social Insurance and Allied Services* might possibly reveal these sentences or parts of sentences, but as a summary of the general thrust of the Report they are a travesty. In summarising Beveridge's intentions in the Report, his biographer, José Harris, wrote in 1977:

> 'For the first time he envisaged that unemployment could be abolished within the context of the existing political system. For the first time he suggested that insurance should be applied uniformly to the whole community and not merely to manual workers or those below a certain income limit. For the first time he proposed that state benefits should provide not merely a platform for private saving but a subsistence income – a subsistence income, moreover, that was geared not merely to physical survival but to current perceptions of "human needs". In the Report of 1942 he laid much greater emphasis than he had previously done on insurance as an instrument of redistribution – as a means not merely of "spreading wages over good times and bad" – but of effecting a positive reallocation of resources from single people to families and from the rich to the poor.'

Such a radical programme provoked strong reactions at the time, which foreshadowed what is being said about the welfare state today. Sir Kingsley Wood, Conservative Chancellor of the Exchequer in the war-time Coalition Government, declared that it was 'ambitious and involves an impracticable financial commitment' and sought by every available means to oppose its acceptance by the Government.

Corelli Barnett, the historian of the period, echoing Kingsley Wood, sees the whole investment in welfare, which he calls the 'New Jerusalem', as the cause of Britain's subsequent decline and concludes his book *The Audit of War* with the following quite remarkably offensive extravagance:

> 'As that descent took its course, the illusions and the dreams of 1945 would fade one by one – the imperial and Commonwealth role, the world power role, British industrial genius, and, at the last, New Jerusalem itself, a dream turned to a dank reality of a segregated, subliterate, unskilled, unhealthy and institutionalised proletariat hanging on the nipple of state maternalism.'

There were many others besides Kingsley Wood who questioned the Beveridge Plan and had not experienced, as working people had, the traumas of unemployment and poverty in the 1930s. When Labour was returned to power, it was determined to right those wrongs, and began at once to implement the Beveridge Report, with much help from Marshall Aid. Two million men and women were demobilised from the armed forces and found employment, but the continuing commitment of forces to Britain's imperial role proved too much to bear through the bitter winter of 1947 and the ending of the American loan in 1948. In the economic difficulties that followed in 1949, it was not, however, the overextended military role that was blamed by Labour's critics, but Beveridge.

A leading Tory, Sir John Anderson, ex-chairman of Vickers and war-time home front supremo, commented in the *News Chronicle* of 1 February 1950 on what Labour was doing, as follows:

'The pace at which family allowances, the increased rate of old age pensions and the vast extension of the old health insurance scheme were introduced was bound to lead to trouble . . .

The reckless haste with which fresh burdens have been assumed, together with the Labour Party's passion for equality, has begun to undermine the foundations of our fiscal system . . .'

By the end of that year the *Daily Mail* (11 October 1950) was quoting the Association of British Chambers of Commerce, calling for immediate steps to economise on the social services:

'In short, the present basis of the social services is designed to discourage work, because the benefits come without working.'

And a Tory MP, Sir Cyril Osborne, writing in the *Grimsby Telegraph* on 5th September, 1949, had already started the long history of complaints about benefit fraud in the administration of social security:

'Social services would be better appreciated and less abused if they had to be paid for . . . We prefer people to depend on their own efforts and not to lean on the State.'

It is the same message from Mr Blair today.

Why Now the Need for Reform?

One part of the argument for welfare reform thus goes back a long way to the continuing choice between bombers and children. Throughout the whole of the post-war period the UK maintained a higher level of military spending as a proportion of national income than any other industrialised country barring only the USA and USSR.

And New Labour is committed to maintaining a military presence including a nuclear capability, the cost of which alone is estimated at £1 billion a year.

Today, the Department of Social Security presents *The Case for Welfare Reform* under the logo of 'Social Security' 'Fifty Years' 'Celebrating the Past' 'Looking to the Future' and refers back to 'Beveridge's Principles', lamenting that

> 'The present system falls a long way short of these principles. Most critically, it is absorbing ever increasing sums of public money, whilst poverty and social exclusion have soared.'

And, amongst the laments we find

> 'Benefit fraud – estimated at £4 billion a year. . .'

> 'The system discourages people from working . . .'

> 'Nearly one million pensioners do not get the Income Support to which they're entitled'

But the old battle for resources and concern for rooting out the 'work-shy' is only part of the rationale for reform. The DSS *Case for Welfare Reform* is less than open about its origins and mentors. These lie in recent United States experience, where the principle of 'workfare' was first generated. This was taken up in a policy review by Neil Kinnock in the late 1980s which established what was called 'a new, humane and balanced ethic that rights must be balanced by responsibilities'. This formula effectively terminated the universal social security principles espoused by Beveridge. In the US life-time welfare benefits are being capped – in some states to two years! Benefits are being moved from people in need to people in work, through the mechanism of Earned Income Tax Credit, from which Mr Brown has taken his Working Families Tax Credit.

So, when New Labour attacks single parents and wriggles around the future of many long established benefits, this is not just because of inherited Tory spending cuts or because Mr Brown believes in even lower public spending levels than the Maastricht Treaty Monetary Union criteria and is keeping to his 'golden rule' of balanced budgets over the economic cycle. Mr Brown is taking credit equally for 'prudence' and for radical innovation, but he is only following the Clinton Government's vision of social security – or social insecurity – from the USA.

The Department of Social Security in presenting its *Case for Welfare Reform* seeks to justify this switch from European to American practice by invoking the authority of Beveridge. In relation to the state pension, for example, they pick on 'Beveridge's desire to see state support of the elderly supplemented by provision by individuals and employees, without revealing Beveridge's prior insistence that the level of benefits should guarantee a universal subsistence income from benefits. This was to be met from contributions by employers, employees and the state, which was operating a progressive tax system. The weakness of the scheme was the absence of any relation to earnings, until SERPS was introduced in 1978, and this lasted only until 1980 when the earnings link for payments was broken again. David Donnison has commented:

'By going at first for a flat rate rather than wage related benefits and contributions, unlike other European countries, the benefits proved too small for richer workers and the contributions too large for the poorer, so that the British social security system languished and private pension schemes prospered.'

This has made it possible for Polly Toynbee to argue the case. 'Secretly behind the scenes', she writes, 'most agree', and she should know,

'national insurance has had its day. It's just another tax, and it's time to end the charade of paying into a non-existent "fund" to get out unspecified but ever dwindling universal benefits that many no longer need. It will take time – but we saw the first step with the announcement that child benefit will be taxed in future. All universal benefits will go that way – last and most politically difficult, the universal pension in these days where one third of pensioners are now very well off and don't need it.'

'The recent Guardian/ICM poll', she goes on, 'shows that most people are quite happy to see child benefit taxed or taken from the well-off. The mystique of universal benefits has gone and people now regard the welfare system as wasteful if it pays out to those who don't need it. This is the beginning of the end of Beveridge, a system designed in another era for a very different and far poorer society, and it never did what it intended any way.'

She was immediately challenged in *The Guardian* by Alan Walker, Professor of Social Policy at Sheffield University, a recognised authority on pensions.

'Polly Toynbee is wrong,' he wrote (*Guardian*, 21.3.98)

'The National Insurance system is not crumbling. The Government may be contemplating its abolition, but it would be foolish. The public still sees a difference between insurance and tax, being more willing to pay the former. There is a "fund", in the sense that receipts from NI can be identified, and it is in healthy surplus. Every other major country in the EU has some form of social insurance. . . With private insurance taking out 25p. in every £1 invested in a pension, why ditch a system that works so efficiently and cheaply?'

Unless you have shares in the insurance companies, he might have added, but instead he gave some suggestions for the future of social insurance which we will consider later.

CHAPTER 5

The DSS Welfare Reform Focus Files

How then does the system now work? What are the arguments for and against it and how does it compare with practice elsewhere in Europe? If you look to the DSS Focus files for the answers, you will be disappointed. They provide a detailed description of all the different benefits under the Social Security system in the UK today, but without any figures for the actual sums paid, except in the case of the disability allowance, which is supposed to be abused and where cuts are proposed. Nor are there any comparisons with European practice, except in the case of Housing Benefit, where again the UK figure is relatively high and is being prepared for the chop. All the emphasis is placed on the rising scale of welfare expenditure (see charts) and on the falling share of the benefits going to the poorest members of society.

The Focus files recognise the great increase in the numbers of unemployed as a reason for rising expenditure – hence the anxiety to get people back into work. But the Focus tables also show the growing number of men seeking early retirement, who will hardly be enticed back to work. They reveal the falling value of the state pension as a major reason for rising poverty. But they do not explain that much of the fall in value is the result of the Tory Government's decision to sever the link between the pension and the growth of average earnings. This decision, which means that a retired couple have lost since 1980 £37 a week on a £100 pension, is not even referred to in the Focus files' 'History of Main Developments since 1948'. This is indeed an economy with the truth. But the file on Pensions is too busy celebrating the recent growth and scale of supplementary private and occupational

1979/80 £49 billion

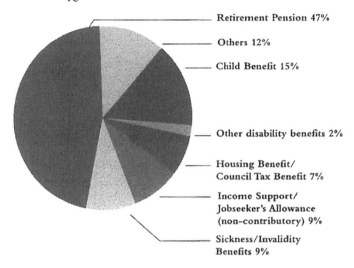

Retirement Pension 47%

Others 12%

Child Benefit 15%

Other disability benefits 2%

Housing Benefit/
Council Tax Benefit 7%

Income Support/
Jobseeker's Allowance
(non-contributory) 9%

Sickness/Invalidity
Benefits 9%

1996/97 £93 billion

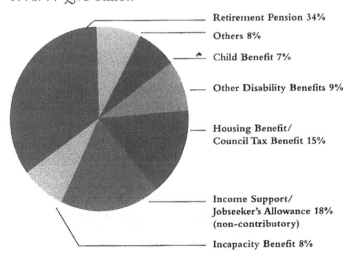

Retirement Pension 34%

Others 8%

Child Benefit 7%

Other Disability Benefits 9%

Housing Benefit/
Council Tax Benefit 15%

Income Support/
Jobseeker's Allowance 18%
(non-contributory)

Incapacity Benefit 8%

Spending has been growing since the start...

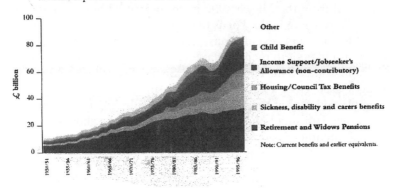

Benefit expenditure 1949/50 to 1996/97

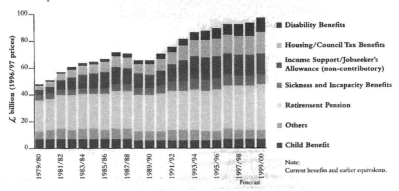

Expenditure on main benefits 1979/80 to 1999/2000

schemes for the minority to be recognising the impoverishment of the majority, let alone mentioning the cases of mis-selling and fraud in private schemes.

The main weakness of the Focus files is that benefits are described and criticised without any reference to the tax system that supports them. We have already seen the working of the system in creating both poverty and income traps. To obtain a picture of the costs and benefits for different income groups of the whole system of social protection, we need to know the effects of taxes as well as benefits on household incomes. This information is available annually in the Government publication, *Economic Trends*, (summarised from the March 1997 issue in Table 2 below); but it is not shown anywhere in the Focus files. Nor is there any information in the files on tax exemptions, farm subsidies, company tax concessions etc., not to mention tax evasion, which must far exceed any benefit fraud. The Focus file on 'Social Security Support for Housing Costs' gives totals of mortgage interest relief and other housing tax reliefs, but there is no breakdown by income groups of beneficiaries. Housing benefit payments also are not shown broken down by income groups, although again this information is available in *Economic Trends*.

Winners and Losers

The thrust of the Focus files is to show that the higher income groups have, since 1979, increased their share of benefit spending at the expense of the poorest. This is demonstrated by the one graph which breaks benefits down by income group. All benefits are lumped together; there is no break down for separate benefits; but the explanation for the declining share of the poorest 20 per cent in total benefits is said to be

> 'the growing number of workless families, increasing non-benefit income for pensioners and the expansion of benefits to meet new needs, such as those of disabled people, irrespective of other sources of income.'

The graph indicates that by far the largest increase over 1979 in share of total benefits has gone to the next-to-the-poorest 20 per cent group. The other three groups have very slightly increased their shares. There is no evidence for the general implication that better off groups are somehow milking the welfare system. The bottom 40 per cent of income recipients still get 60 per cent of the benefits. Apart from the pensioners and the unemployed, the largest area of benefit growth has been in sickness, disability and carers' benefits. These are not means tested and the largest single element (44 per cent) in these benefits is Incapacity Benefit, which is based upon National Insurance Contributions. Both the last

Government and New Labour have targeted these benefits for reductions, in order to encourage those who are disabled to seek work. This cannot apply to about a half who are over 65; and the quarter who are between 45 and 65 will find it very difficult to get jobs, especially in areas of high unemployment.

Housing benefit is another benefit which has been increasing as a share of the total. The Focus files state that this 'reflects the deregulation of private sector rents in 1989 and longer term reduction in direct subsidies to the rented sector.' Benefit is in fact a fairly straight substitute for subsidies. Mortgage relief goes mainly to better off families, but according to the *Economic Trends* figures, housing benefit goes almost entirely to the lowest income groups. There has been much talk in the press about the need to reduce housing benefit, with Frank Dobson reminding us that it costs as much as a quarter of the NHS budget. But it is generally agreed that, without a major reorganisation of housing finance and increased public sector building, the problem will remain.

If Mr Blair complains that Social Security takes more public money than Health, Education and Law and Order combined, it is worth reminding him of the close connection between the needs that give rise to this public spending and of the relation between taxes paid and benefits, both in cash and in kind, received. It is possible that because of the large number of old people in the lower income groups and the spending by the rich on private health care, that the NHS is most heavily used by the poorer groups. This may also be true of education for non-retired households, because there are more children in the lower income groups and they do not use private schools. But we should need to know the take up by income groups of places in grammar schools and in higher education, especially in the most expensive areas like medical schools. The Dearing Committee showed that access to higher education was privileged, but did not give figures by income group for the payment of grants, prior to the introduction of fees. It is impossible to make any kind of judgement of the costs and benefits for the country as a whole and for different groups without adequate statistical evidence; and this the Focus files do not supply.

Social Security in Relation to National Income

The aim of a comprehensive study of the whole welfare system including the basis of taxation and National Insurance Contributions should not be to justify the making of savings here or there, which seems to lie behind so much of the Government's presentation and of the Focus files highly selective statistics. It should be genuinely to seek to find a fairer distribution of all the costs and benefits so as to reduce the inequalities that deform our society. The statement of *The Case for Welfare Reform* by the DSS proclaims that 'Reform will be driven by our principles, not cuts led.' But what are their principles? What cuts will follow their pursuit, even if they do not lead the reforms? A *Guardian* report (5.1.98) that £3.27 billions are to be cut from the welfare budget this year was subsequently corrected in the details but not in the substance. £3.3 billions out of a total budget of £90 billions is not a large sum, although Mr Blair evidently regards the £3.5 billion windfall tax on the privatised utilities 'for welfare into work' schemes as big enough to indicate his seriousness in tackling long-term unemployment.

Most of the information and the graphs in the Focus files give a quite false impression of the scale of the increases of expenditure that are spelt out page by page and file by file. This is because they are not related to the growth over time of the whole national income. On page 3 of file 01, for example, our hair is made to stand on end by the claim that since 1949/50, the first full year of the Beveridge social security system, 'the cost of provision has risen nearly eightfold in real terms' from £12 billion in 1996/7 prices to presumably nearly £96 billion. This is not even accurate. If housing subsidies are included in the 1949/50 figure, as Housing Benefit is in the 1996/7 figure on the chart, then Social Security spending in 1949/50 at 1996/7 prices would be £18.5 billions, and not £12 billions; and the Focus file itself gives a total for 1996/7 of £92 billions and not £96 billions. 92 is five times 18.5 and not eight times. Moreover, during this period the national income rose threefold. Spending on Social Security and Housing rose from 22 per cent to 32 per cent of government expenditure and from 8 per cent to 16 per cent of national income (Table 1.) This is effectively a doubling of provision, but it has to be related to both income and

Table 1
UK Government Expenditure 1948-96
as % of GNP and by sectors as % of totals

ITEM	1948	1958	1968	1978	1984	1996
GNP (£ billions)	11.8	22.8	43.8	168	326	742
(1990 prices)	188	240	335	421	451	602
Govt. spending						
(£ billions)	4.2	8.3	19.1	72	147	306
Govt. % of GNP	35.5	36.4	43.6	42.8	45.1	41.2
Shares of Govt. (%)						
Debt Interest	10.8	11.2	10.0	10.4	10.7	8.8
Military	18	15.5	12.8	10.4	8.0	7.0
Other	23.8	29.1	27.2	28.9	27.1	23.2
Education	8.3	10.8	12.8	12.0	11.2	12.0
Social security	15.6	17.8	21.2	22.7	26.8	28.0
Housing	6.7	2.0	1.6	1.6	3.0	4.0
Health	7.2	13.6	14.4	14.0	13.2	17.0
Food subsidies	9.6	–	–	–	–	–
Agriculture	1.5	4.0	1.3	..	..	..

Notes: Agricultural subsidies are included in 'Other' after 1975 and appear in the payments to the European Union. GNP at market prices.
Sources: *National Income & Expenditure* Blue Books 1966-76 and *Economic Trends*, 1979 and *Annual Supplement*, 1997 and CSO, *Annual Abstract of Statistics*, 1996, Table 3.1.

expenditure changes over the years. If food (and farm) subsidies in 1949 are added to the sum of social security and housing expenditure, then the difference between 1949 and 1996 practically disappears, since these subsidies contributed over 10 per cent to the shares of government expenditure.

Combining Taxes and Benefits

To get a true picture of the working of the welfare system, it is necessary to combine the impact of benefits and taxes on different income groups. The articles in *Economic Trends* on income distribution by quintile groups before and after cash benefits and taxes show the trends over time. Table 2 below summarises the changes between 1977 and 1995/6 and includes figures for 1987 when there was a change of trend. What the Table reveals is a clear decline in the share of the bottom group over the period, in original income, in gross income, that is after the receipt of cash benefits,

Table 2
Shares (%) of UK Incomes: Before and After Benefits and Taxes, by
Quintile Income Groups, 1977, 1987, 1995/6 and 1996/7

Income share	Year	Bottom	4th	3rd	2nd	Top	All
Original Income	1977	3.6	10	18	26	43	100
	1987	2.1	7	16	25	50	100
	1995/6	2.6	7	15	25	50	100
	1996/7	2.0	7	15	25	51	100
Gross Income	1977	8.9	13	18	24	37	100
after benefits	1987	7.5	11	16	23	43	100
	1995/6	7.4	11	16	23	43	100
	1996/7	7.0	11	16	23	44	100
Post-Tax Income	1977	9.4	14	17	23	37	100
	1987	7.6	12	16	22	43	100
	1995/6	6.9	12	16	23	43	100
	1996/7	7.0	11	16	22	44	100

Note: *Economic Trends,* March 1997, p.53, and March 1998, p.35.
Source: Figures don't add up to 100 because of rounding.

and in post tax income. The gainers have been those in the top group, partly as the result of more unequal incomes and partly as the result of Mrs Thatcher's tax cuts for higher income earners. There has been no addition in cash benefits for the lower income groups to make up for that. Indeed the share of cash benefits taken by the bottom group falls steadily, i.e. the difference between original income and gross income (8.9 - 3.6 = 5.3 in 1977 and 7.4 - 2.6 = 4.8 in 1995/6 – see Table 2).

There cannot be any doubt from a perusal of Table 2 that inequalities have been growing over the last two decades and welfare provision has simply failed to correct this despite increases in state expenditure. The reasons are chiefly the massive rise in the numbers of unemployed and the numbers taking early retirement, on the one hand, and the fact of an ageing population structure, on the other. But the rise in the original income share of the top quintile, continuing in the latest tables for 1996/7, and the fall in the lowest quintile's share, suggest fundamental inequalities in wealth and power.

Over the whole period from 1949 to 1996 the numbers of unemployed rose from 300,000 to around 2 million and reached well over 3 million in the 1980s (and these figures understate the total workless by another million). The Focus file on Unemployment reports that between 1979 and 1996, households with working age adults but no one at work rose from 9 per cent of all households to 21 per cent. This means far more people in need of other benefits – income support, housing benefit, council tax benefit and disability allowances – since the disabled are the least likely to get work when jobs are scarce – and needing benefits for much longer periods, all associated with absence of employment. Since 1979 the poorest households have seen their post-tax incomes fall not only as a share of total incomes but almost, if not quite, absolutely.

The Creation of Unemployment

The Focus files refer to these changes as 'social and demographic changes outside the benefit system' (file 0.1, p.10), but the rise of workless households is not an exogenous factor. Beveridge's proposals were designed to end unemployment by ensuring a more equal distribution of income. He accepted, indeeed he helped to develop, the Keynesian view that full employment could be achieved by increased government spending. This view is pilloried today, as a failed form of throwing money at a problem, but the aim was to increase the purchasing power of the poor, so as to maintain demand for the extra goods and services which increased productivity was making available. Without state intervention, too much of the result of the new productivity went into profits, which did not necessarily lead to lower prices and increased consumption or even to more investment.

This argument became unfashionable when it was overtaken by monetarists determined to protect the value of money against inflation, and when the medium to small nation state proved unable to protect the private capital in its borders from global flight to places where taxes and government spending were less rigorous and wages were lower. The argument has, however, been revived recently among economic experts, but not inside New Labour. The authors of the UN Development Programme *Human Development Report, 1997* have been revealing the world-wide connection between unequal income distribution and slow growth rates leading to unemployment and poverty. The UN Conference on Trade and Development in its annual surveys of *Trade and Development* for 1995, 1996 and 1997 criticised government policies that were based on monetary restrictions and reduced government spending.The International Labour Organisation in its 1996/7 *World Development Report* asked the question whether 'Full Employment is Passé' and concluded that there were no arguments from the facts of globalisation that could properly be used to stop governments taking joint action to re-establish full employment. The most distinguished group of British economists, the Clare Group, decided in 1995 that it was possible once again 'to think the unthinkable' and to 'promote full employment as an objective of government policy', using government measures to maintain aggregate demand for goods and services (National Institute *Economic Review*, February 1995.)

The Keynesian argument has reached out beyond the economists to be taken up in the European Parliament in two reports endorsed by overwhelming majorities. Both contained proposals for joint and common action by governments and the European Union to generate funds through a Union borrowing facility like the United States federal capacity, to support employment projects throughout the Union. The proposals have been held up by the anxieties of the Finance Ministers of several states, and particularly of Great Britain, that such borrowing would conflict with the aims of fiscal convergence set for membership of Economic and Monetary Union (EMU) in the Maastricht Agreement. In fact, by creating a federal fund the aim was precisely to by-pass the Maastricht limitations.

Most of the member states have in the event been cutting back on their measures of social protection in order to comply with the Maastricht criteria. The UK having already a much lower level of public spending than the others has not needed to make such extensive cuts. But the danger of a Dutch auction to offer global capital the lowest taxes and the least regulated economy as well as the lowest wages and employers' charges has become a reality with New Labour in the lead to deregulate. How far the UK is already below the other European states in the matter of social protection will become clear later.

Increased Numbers of the Elderly

In an important sense New Labour's plans for the future of the Welfare State hang on its proposals for old people. We have already noted that the breaking of the link between the growth of average earnings and the annual increase in the pension has steadily reduced the pension's value and is set to reduce it still further in future. Yet there are no proposals for re-establishing the link – either for the basic state pension or for the State Earnings Related Pension, after it is fixed on retirement. It is said that the cost would be far too great in view of the growing number of old people in the population. This is made much of in the Focus files, and there is no doubt that the proportion of what, in spite of all their contributions, are called 'dependents' in the population is rising, and after 2010 will rise faster than the population of working age. From then on, instead of there being 3.4 men and women of working age to one retired person, the so-called 'support ratio' will fall by 2030 to two to one.

Why should this be a serious problem? If productivity continues to increase, working hours in a life time should be reduced. Much of the pressure on pension funds is due to the increasing numbers of men and women taking early retirement. The problem only arises because increases in productivity are not translated into shorter hours for all or into higher incomes for the poor from which savings can be made for old age. Some have more work than ever and higher earnings, others have none. The population is ageing as birth rates fall but also as people live longer. The number of men and women of pensionable age in the UK rose between 1951 and 1996 from 6.8 million to 10.7 million, that is from 13.6 per cent to 16.8 per cent of the population, and the average expectation of life rose over roughly the same period from 67 years for men and 74 for women to 74 years for men, 79 for women. Instead of having only a few years of retirement, men as well as women can have as many as 10 to 20 years. More old people living longer inevitably make more demands for support, not only of pension income but of help with other needs to meet increasing disablement. It is the same everywhere; there is no sudden unexplained increase in needs particular to the UK.

The DSS Focus files concentrate their attention on *average* pensioners' incomes, which have more than kept pace with earnings, rising from under to well over half of average earnings. But this is because of the increase in personal and occupational pensions that provide a second tier to the state pension. By 1995/6 over two thirds of pensioners had some form of second-tier provision compared with only 45 per cent in 1979. The result is great inequalities: the top 10 per cent of pensioners in 1995/6 had an average income of over £600 a week, while the bottom 10 per cent had only £70. Pensioners make up one quarter of the poorest 20 per cent of the population. Income support, disablement allowance, housing and other benefits have become a necessity for them and a million men and women who are eligible for these benefits, it appears, choose not to take them up.

Government spokesmen have stated that they will try to discover the causes of the failure to take up help that is available, but there is no suggestion of raising the value of the state pension or of improving the SERPS to attract more contributors. The Focus file does not reveal that the private pensions currently cost the Treasury £9.3 billion, equivalent to over a quarter of the cost of the basic state pension. Neither does it reveal the risks and high administrative costs of private pension provision, nor the fact that most occupational pensions cannot be carried over from job to job.The idea that is being mooted of making the contribution to private pension schemes compulsory, which Mr Field says that he is 'considering seriously', makes absolutely no sense for the low paid. Deductions made by the employer from the pay cheque for private and mutual providers may be possible, although extremely wasteful, for those on higher incomes, but they are prohibitive for those on lower incomes who make up the great majority of those not now making pension contributions.

Increasing Disablement

The Focus files show that the proportion of the population reporting themselves having a long standing illness, disability or infirmity has not increased very much over the last twenty years, and nearly half of those reporting are over 65 years of age. Of the ones who are under 50 over half are economically active. On the other hand, the numbers of men and women receiving incapacity benefit has risen from around 400,000 threefold to 1.2 million over the same period. Expenditure doubled up to 1995/6 when changes were made in the rules for eligibility. The Government is now proposing even stricter tests for new claimants, which will be based upon the scale of their employability. In Annexe 2, examples are given of cases already affected by the previous Government's tightening up of criteria. Disability living allowances are to remain national and universal, and not means tested or farmed out to local authorities. But real term cuts are proposed, with benefits concentrated on those with the greatest disability.

The Focus files claim that sickness and disability are now the most common reason for adults in workless households being out of work; and the comment follows that 'An increasing number of families without any one in work means more people have become dependent on social security benefits.' The increasing number of workless families is explained partly because of smaller family size, partly because of increased unemployment in areas of declining industry (coal, ship-building, engineering), where men have been liable to sustain industrial injuries, where no alternative job opportunities for men have been created and where there was always a lack of jobs for women. Early retirement has become for many the only option, and as people live longer, the length and needs of disability increase.

It used to be a matter of pride that British society was to some extent civilised, having a certain sense of security and serenity, as Nye Bevan used to claim for it. It hasn't that sense now. We are told that we are having to compete in the tough markets of the world and social protection is a burden both on the employer and the tax payer. One might then have expected that the Focus files would have comparative statistics on the measures of social protection in other countries. In fact the only comparative tables or graphs compare workless households in different countries in 1994 as a percentage of all households and the incidence of lone parenthood by age and employment. In relation to workless households only Belgium, Spain and Ireland are shown to have higher proportions than the UK. In relation to lone parenthood the UK is shown to have one of the highest proportions, and the youngest in age, of comparable countries.

These are selective statistics to prove a point. We need to look at all the other comparative figures for social protection, not only of numbers of claimants but of government expenditures, before we can judge whether UK levels are so much higher than elsewhere as to cause concern. This we shall do, and the fact we shall find is that the UK is on almost every count at the very bottom of the league in social protection among European countries and often also among a wider selection of developed countries. Yet, in the Focus file 02 on 'The Evolution of Social Security' (page 8), the authors have the audacity to claim that 'In Europe a number of countries have followed the UK in encouraging the development of private provision of pensions . . . policies in other areas mirror and develop moves in the UK'. But they have to admit that elsewhere: 'Not all changes are away from state provision.'

CHAPTER 6

Mr Blair's Road Show

'Reform' is a big word with two possible meanings: to restore something to its original form, and to make it into a new form. The Reformation and reformism appealed to this ambiguity, but reform came to be used in the Nineteenth Century in opposition to revolution, as a description of an amendment rather than a total change in society. Reform Acts in Britain gave votes to extra groups of the population. They did not fundamentally change the constitution. Nonetheless they were preceded by much deliberation and a thorough examination of the current situation and of the changes proposed. Mr Blair is seeking to reform the welfare state in Britain, because he believes that it is excessively costly, out of date and no longer meeting the needs of the poorest people. But there has been no Royal Commission or grand debate on the issue. Mr Blair's 'road show' is less a consultation than a crusade for a policy he is advocating. The nearest approach to an Inquiry was the Commission on Social Justice set up by the late John Smith and chaired by Sir Gordon Borrie, which reported in 1994.

Rejection of the Borrie Report

By the time the Report was published, Tony Blair had become leader of the Labour Party, and he greeted the Report in the following words:

> 'John Smith's anger at the state of Britain today led him to establish the Commission on Social Justice. Its report will inform Labour's policy making and provide the basis for a vital national debate about the future of work and welfare. It is essential reading for everyone who wants a new way forward for our country.'

Since then, we have not heard much reference to the Report, except in the sound-bites where Mr Blair draws upon the rhetoric of its basic propositions, but rejects the conclusions:

'• we must transform the welfare state from a safety net in times of trouble to a spring board for economic opportunity;
• we must improve access to education and training, and invest in the talent of all our people;
• we must promote real choices across the life-cycle for men and women in the balance of employment, family, education, leisure and retirement;
• we must reconstruct the social wealth of our country . . .'

Although the Borrie report came out in favour of social insurance it was weak on the continuing need for redistribution, caricaturing those who still believe in Old Labour's commitment to greater equality as 'Levellers' (many would not object!) and as 'pessimists who do not believe in the possibility of full employment' (when that belief is their main claim to differentiation from New Labour). The Report made much of the changes in society – more indivualism, smaller families, more women at work – and changes in work patterns – more job moves in a lifetime, earlier retirement – some of which, as we shall see, can be questioned, but which Mr Blair has seized on in his argument for reform.

While the Report supported the social insurance principle, it drew back from the universal principle, fearing the cost involved. But it was highly critical of the 'apostles of a deregulated Britain.' Now this, in the event, is what Mr Blair has become, proselytizing not only for the conversion of Britain but of the whole of Europe. The Report, however, proposed the idea of an 'investors' Britain', which Mr Blair has seized upon. This is apparently to be just what it sounds like, a paradise for those with capital, who are to be the sponsors on the welfare reform 'road show'. Investment in job creation is only to be a part of New Labour's new society, in so far as it makes young men and women more 'employable' under 'welfare to work' projects, by reducing welfare payments and deregulating wages and conditions of work. Investment is for big business.

Mr Blair's Case for Reform

So what are Mr Blair's arguments for reform in the welfare state? At their centre is the insidious suggestion that the availability of welfare 'hand-outs', as he calls them, is itself the cause of the unacceptably high level of unemployment. This was the argument for cutting the benefit entitlement of lone parents and retaining the last of the Tory Government cuts, that of the disablement and incapacity payments. The alternative view, of course, would be that it is the lack of jobs that forces people onto welfare. But Mr Blair's criticisms of the whole existing structure of welfare provision went very much further in his article in *The Times* of January 5th, 1998. The proposals he made were not just reformist but counter-revolutionary, based on so-called facts about the current welfare system which Professor Townsend (*Tribune*, 13.02.98) regards as mere 'fancies', which can all be challenged:

1. The welfare state is imposing a 'growing cost to ordinary tax payers', costing 'each family £80 a week', and social security now exceeding spending on 'health, education and law and order combined'.

2. Some 'savings' must be found soon in the much increased bill, and 'not after several years', especially in the field of pensions.

3. More is spent on 'disability and incapacity benefit than . . . on the whole school system'

4. The welfare state subsidises the rich, who do not need its benefits and does not reach 'a million poor pensioners entitled to income support' and leaves 'four million children living in poverty'.

5. It is plagued by 'benefit fraud, estimated at £4 billion a year'.

6. It creates perverse incentives – 360,000 people face an effective tax rate of 80 per cent or higher on withdrawal of benefits, when they enter work.

7. It is so complex that people do not understand how much better off they would be by working;

8. So, it provides ' welfare and not work' - for young people, lone mothers, the disabled - 'many of whom can work and want to work'.

Then Mr Blair adds a number of positive points, many of which are correct and need to be taken into account in any changes in the system, but do not justify the general line of the reforms he is advancing:

9. It needs to be adapted to changing life styles: 'more women working', 'changing jobs – at least 6 or 7 times in a life time' - changing partners - 'more marriages ending in divorce'.

10. It should aim to 'extend opportunity' and to 'narrow social division' as well as to relieve poverty.

11. It should, at the same time, 'spend taxpayers' money wisely'.

12. It should 'guarantee' to 'support those who are in genuine need', 'those most in need'.

Mr Blair also said that changes will be 'based on the same principles' as 'Beveridge's in 1945 . . . that successfully tackles poverty, and provides security and opportunity at points in your life when you need it most'. Now, it is necessary to remind Mr Blair that the Beveridge principles discussed earlier were principles of universality, and not of providing a safety net for the targeted most-in-need. As John Gray has argued (*Guardian*, January 26, 1998) that way, providing a safety net with no benefits for the tax payers, lies the danger of continuing refusal of 'Middle England' to pay up for state spending, and thus continuing encouragement to them to opt for private provision in place of state services. The divided England that Mr Blair bemoans would indeed become a reality, divided between those who can afford private pensions, private medicine, private schooling for their childen and other private insurances and those who fall into the national safety net. It is not a pretty picture, and if the cost to the tax payer of health and education and social security falls, the cost of law and order will certainly rise.

Is the Cost of Welfare Growing Out of Control?

More than this, the whole Blair package is based upon a blatant misrepresentation of the existing welfare provision. This becomes clear as soon as we look at the actual facts and compare Britain's welfare state today with what it was in the past and with similar provision throughout Europe. We can then answer the ten points listed above one by one, as we go along.

What is the actual cost of welfare in Britain today? This is said by Mr Blair to be £80 per family per week, and growing. We can first take the point about growth and about social security spending now exceeding that on education, health and law and order. Spending on social security obviously rises and falls with levels of unemployment, since payments for the unemployed account for at least a tenth of the social security budget.

There is some evidence here of a rising trend, but even using the National Institute for Economic and Social Research (NIESR) standardised unemployment rate and not the claimant rate, this certainly underestimates the numbers of unemployed towards the end

Table 3

Year	1984	1985	1986	1987	1988	1989	1990
Unemployed rate (%)	11.7	11.2	11.2	10.3	8.6	7.2	6.9
Social security % of GDP	12.0	11.8	11.8	11.0	10.6	10.0	10.4
Year	1991	1992	1993	1994	1995	1996	1997
Unemployed rate (%)	8.8	10.1	10.4	9.6	8.5	7.6	6.0
Social security % of GDP	12.0	13.1	13.4	13.1	12.8	12.0	10.0

Note & Source: Umemployed rate = standardised rate from National Institute *Economic Review* Social security expenditure % of GDP at market prices from CSO, *Annual Abstract of Statistics.*

of the period. According to the Unemployment Unit, the rates in 1993 and 1994 should have been between 12.5 per cent and 13 per cent. The 6 per cent figure for 1997, as already mentioned, would be just over 10 per cent. Most of those unemployed who are excluded from the claimant count would still be receiving forms of support – through early retirement, redundancy payments, sickness and disability allowances. Indeed, it is part of Mr Blair's case that such welfare payments are preventing them from seeking employment. Others like the social scientists working with the Coalfield Communities Campaign, who have studied closely what is happening in areas where the coal industry and other industries have been closed down, know that it is the absolute absence of jobs that forces people to turn to welfare (see Ken Coates, MEP & Michael Barratt Brown, *Community Under Attack*, Spokesman, 1997).

As Ivan Turok and David Webster have argued in *Local Economy* (February 1998) in relation to 'welfare to work' schemes, people and vacancies can be matched in the Home Counties, where vacancies are plentiful, but not where they are lacking. 'The priority in high unemployment areas', they conclude, 'must be to create additional jobs'. Already, in these areas, there are prematurely retired workers who would take up work again if there were the jobs. Professor Townsend has calculated that the direct cost in benefits of premature retirement is £7 billion, due to 850,000 more men in their fifties and early sixties being prematurely retired and another 450,000 being unemployed since 1979. The state pensions bill in 1996 was £30 billion.

'The Government does not care to number the prematurely retired among the unemployed', he adds.

The facts about expenditures on health and education and law and order are that the first two combined have always been roughly equivalent to the expenditure on social security. Before the 1980s social security took somewhat less than the others combined, although this depends on whether you include food subsidies. Since the 1980s, as unemployment rates have risen (from 5 per cent to 10 per cent), and early retirement has grown apace, social security expenditure including housing benefit has taken somewhat more. Even with recent falls in unemployment and with higher expenditures on health and education, the reduction has been small (Table 1 above). Why Mr Blair should throw in the cost of law and order is not clear. It would certainly rise if social security suffered heavy cuts without new employment.

CHAPTER 7

Who Pays for the Welfare State?

Taxes and Benefits Compared

Mr Blair said that on average every family was paying £80 a week for the Welfare State. That is certainly a large sum, over £4000 a year. But is it a correct estimate and for which families? According to the latest survey of 'The Effects of Taxes and Benefits upon Household Income' (*Economic Trends*, March 1997) an average non-retired household of two adults and a child in 1995-6 was paying about £10,000 in taxes and NIC and receiving £2500 in cash benefits and £3000 of benefits in kind. Now Mr Blair may mean by welfare what appears from the text as only the cash benefits. Such social security payments were then taking somewhat under a third of all government expenditure, so that the average non-retired household was paying out around £3000 towards social security and receiving the £2500 in cash benefits. Of course the households where there were no unemployed would be receiving less in cash benefits and paying more in tax (£5300 of the average £10,000 tax paid would have been in income tax and NIC, the rest in VAT etc).

Combining Taxes and Benefits

If Mr Blair means to include the benefits in kind, mainly for education and health, then the average non-retired household receives another £3000 a year and pays for this another third of the £10,000 in taxes and National Insurance. It is very hard to see how Mr Blair can find a figure of £4000 per family (the £80 a week) being paid for cash benefits let alone for benefits in kind. Only families in the top 20 per cent of non-retired households, with over £40,000 a year, would be paying net taxes on average of more than £12,000 so that they could be

Table 4
Average value of cash benefits for each quintile group of NON-RETIRED households, 1995-96

	Quintile groups of NON-RETIRED households ranked by equivalised disposable income					All non-retired house-holds
	Bottom	2nd	3rd	4th	Top	holds
Average per household (£ per year)						
Contributory						
Retirement pension	100	400	340	310	220	270
Incapacity benefit	390	430	280	270	90	290
Unemployment benefit	70	50	40	20	20	40
Other	60	80	60	100	90	80
Total contributory	620	960	730	710	420	690
Non-Contributory						
Income support	1,850	690	220	80	40	570
Child benefit	710	510	420	310	220	430
Housing benefits	1,290	620	170	40	10	430
Sickness/disablement related	140	420	280	160	70	210
Other	360	310	130	100	40	190
Total non-contributory	4,340	2,540	1,220	680	390	1,830
Total cash benefits	4,960	3,500	1,940	1,400	800	2,520
Cash benefits as a percentage of gross income	57	23	9	5	2	11
Gross Income (£s)	8,700	15,150	21,500	28,000	40,000	23,060

Note: Figures don't add up because of rounding.
Source: *Economic Trends,* March 1997, p.53.

Table 5
Income tax, employees' NIC and Local taxes[2] as percentages of gross income quintile group of NON-RETIRED households, 1995-96

	Quintile groups of NON-RETIRED households ranked by equivalised disposable income					All non-retired house-holds
	Bottom	2nd	3rd	4th	Top	holds
Percentages						
Income tax[1]	7.8	9.0	12.2	14.6	18.8	14.6
Employees' NIC	2.0	4.3	5.3	5.4	4.4	4.6
Local taxes[2]	6.7	4.1	3.2	2.5	1.8	2.9
Total	16.5	17.4	20.6	22.5	25.0	22.0
Indirect taxes	26.4	20.9	18.4	15.5	11.6	16.2

[1] After tax relief at source on mortgage interest and life assurance premiums.
[2] Gross Council tax, Domestic rates and Water charges but after deducting discounts and Council tax transitional relief.

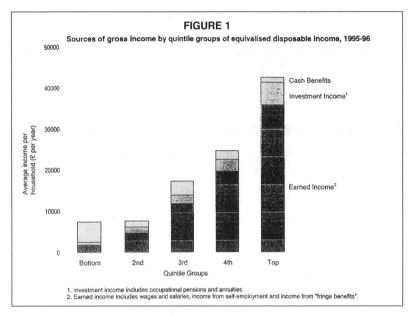

FIGURE 1

Sources of gross income by quintile groups of equivalised disposable income, 1995-96

1. Investment income includes occupational pensions and annuities.
2. Earned income includes wages and salaries, income from self-employment and income from "fringe benefits".

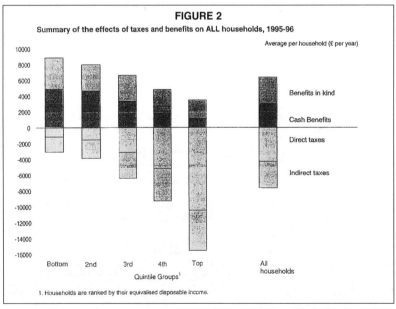

FIGURE 2

Summary of the effects of taxes and benefits on ALL households, 1995-96

1. Households are ranked by their equivalised disposable income.

80

contributing as much as a third or £80 a week to welfare benefits. (see figure 1.) Perhaps Mr Blair was thinking of his own tax bill.

It is an important argument of Mr Blair's, supported by the Focus files, that since 1979 the share of social security benefits received by the poorest 20 per cent of households has fallen from over 40 per cent to 30 per cent of the total, while all other household quintiles have gained. The reason must be in part the fall in the relative value of the state pension since it was delinked from average earnings.

Pensioners make up one quarter of the lowest 20 per cent of households in shares of national incomes, according to the Focus files (33 per cent according to *Economic Trends*, March 1997, Table B, p.29). Most retired people are, however, not in the lowest income group. This is because of SERPS ('due for the chop', according to Professor Townsend) and of private and occupational pensions.

The lowest income group is largely made up of the unemployed and unoccupied, and increasingly of economically active people on very low pay. These non-retired households, which make up the three quarters or two thirds of the bottom quintile, are shown in the annual statements of 'The Effects of Taxes and Benefits upon Household Incomes', published in *Economic Trends*, as suffering the most extraordinary burden of taxation. While 57 per cent of their gross income consists of cash benefits (Table 4), they are paying on average 16.5 per cent of this income in income tax, NIC and local taxes, plus another 26 per cent in indirect taxes (Table 5). In other words, on average they receive about £5000 gross income per year in benefits and pay £3740 in taxes and contributions. This is the poverty crunch and figures for households conceal the poverty of married women, where there is only one household income.

This is where the welfare state needs reform, but it is in the tax system and wages system more than in the benefits system. At present the tax system in the UK is highly regressive. While it takes more in taxation in money from the rich than the poor (see fig 1.), it does not take a *higher proportion* of the income of the rich. In fact it takes a lower proportion, even if we calculate the proportion of gross income, that is after cash benefits but not benefits in kind are included with original income (Table 6 below).

The fact that the bottom income group pays so much in tax reflects the penalty in tax liability that arises if unemployed workers move into

Table 6
UK Taxes and Benefits of Households:
By Income Group in Quantiles, 1995-6 with a comparison of 1977

A. Original Income and Gross Income (£s) and Taxes

Income Group	Bottom	4th	3rd	2nd	Top	All
Original Income	2,430	6,090	13,790	22,450	41,260	17,200
Cash Benefits	4,910	4,660	3,360	2,130	1,190	3,250
Gross Income	7,340	10,750	17,150	24,580	42,450	20,450
All Taxes	3,060	3,860	6,420	9,270	15,560	7,640
Post-Tax Income	4,280	6,890	10,730	15,310	26,890	12,820

B. Taxes/Benefits % of Original Income

Direct Taxes and NIC	46	25	23	23	25	25
Indirect taxes	79	34	34	18	12	20
Total Taxes	125	59	57	41	37	45
Cash Benefits	205	80	25	9	3	23
Benefits in Kind	162	55	23	12	5.5	18

C. Taxes as % of

Gross Income 1995	41.5	36	37.5	37.5	36.6	37.5
Gross Income 1977	28	36	35.5	35.5	36.5	35

Sources: for 1995/6: 'Effects of Taxes and Benefits upon Household Income, 1995-6', *Economic Trends*, March 1997, p.29; for 1977: *Economic Trends*, January 1979

low paid employment – the poverty trap, already discussed. This is particularly evident in Table 5 which gives figures of taxes for non-retired households. Mr Brown has been talking about a 10 per cent rate of tax for low incomes. In its effect this would mainly hit single, childless tax-payers, because others have married couple plus personal allowances up to the income where the 10 per cent band would stop. What is needed is a decent statutory minimum wage; plus the restoration of higher rates of tax for higher incomes, which the Thatcher Governments cancelled, and New Labour seems to be reluctant to reimpose for fear of losing the support of the contented classes. From Table 5 we can see that the top income group pays the lowest proportion of their incomes in combined direct and indirect taxes of any groups of non-retired households.

Even when the retired households are included (as in Table 6), the top income group only contributes the same proportion of household income in taxes as the average household, and the bottom income group is almost as heavily taxed. The inequalities arise from the extremely regressive nature of indirect taxation (VAT etc.), the poorest group paying a higher proportion of their gross income in indirect taxes than the richest group. Under the Thatcher Governments, indirect taxes were raised while direct taxes were lowered. The last lines of Table 6 indicate the result.

A Regressive Tax System

The fact is that the tax system has become much more regressive in the last twenty years so as quite to offset the increase in social security payments, as the last two lines of Table 6 reveal.

There has been an increase in the tax take on middle incomes, but the top income group today no longer pays even above the household average as it did 20 years ago. The main change is the big *increase* in the levy on the very poorest households – from 28 per cent of their gross income to a monstrous 41 per cent. It is true that we are not entirely comparing like with like, because of the change in household structure. The households today in every income group have fewer members (average 2.5 instead of 3.5 as in 1977) and in particular only one child on average even in the non-retired households. This would imply fewer earners and because of the increase in lone parent families more benefit receivers. But the poorest groups have in fact changed least, having the largest number of members per family (3.3 on average) of any group of the non-retired households and the largest number of members (2.7 on average) of any group among all households.

If we go further back then beyond the last decade, the idea of a large growth in the taxation of ordinary households in the UK for costly social payments is not what the facts reveal. The tax bill has risen considerably, but not chiefly because of social security payments, and the incidence of taxation has moved very sharply down the income groups. We can take the year 1977 as a bench mark, because this was the last year before the Callaghan and Thatcher cuts in welfare spending. If, now, instead of comparing the tax take with gross income, i.e. after receipt of cash benefits, we compare cash benefits and taxes with original income of all non-retired households, the increase both in cash benefits and in tax take are obvious (Table 7.). But the share of original income taken by taxes to finance social security payments (14 per cent) is still slightly above the cash benefits received (11.7 per cent).

Table 7
All Non-Retired Households
Taxes and Benefits share of Original Income, 1977 and 1995-96

Year	Non-retired Household Original Income £s 1995 values	Benefits-Received		Taxes Paid			
		Cash	Kind	Direct	Indirect	Total	for Soc. Sec.
1977	16,000	7.5	15.5	19.5	18.0	37.5	9
1995-6	21,450	11.7	15.4	25.0	19.5	44.5	14

Notes: 1995 values means 1977 incomes adjusted for 1995 prices
Direct taxes include National Insurance payments
Share of payment going to Social Security includes housing payment.
Sources: Economic Trends, Annual supplements and *Economic Trends*, January 1979 and March 1997.

There is some distribution taking place from the employed and advantaged to the unemployed and disadvantaged, although, as we have seen, redistribution from rich to poor has been reduced.

It is necessary to recognise that households without any unemployed would be receiving less benefits and paying more tax, which is in part clear from the figures comparing 1977, when unemployment was only 4.5 per cent, and 1995 when it was at twice that level. All average figures of tax payments, however, have to be considered in the light of the opportunities of richer households for tax avoidance, through self employed expense accounts and other small business tax reliefs and mortgage relief, not to mention tax evasion through offshore trust investments. Furthermore, in so far as a proportion of public spending is financed through borrowing, it will be the richer households which will be benefiting by members lending money to the Government and the poorer who will be contributing to paying the interest on the debt. Mr Blair does not mention that the Government has been paying out each year throughout the 1980s and early 1990s almost as much in debt interest as it was for education.

Welfare Costs and National Income

The most important comment to make on the claim that welfare is costing too much is that the national income is now twice what it was in real terms 30 years ago and three times what it was 50 years ago. One might have supposed that a richer society would have been able to afford a larger proportion of its income for education and health and the

84

needs of the old and disadvantaged. Up to the 1970s this appears to have been what was happening, but thereafter the increases have been slight and have been following the rise and fall of unemployment, as we have already seen. What has changed, moreover, has been the shift of taxation from the rich to the poor, so that they have increasingly been paying for their own benefits. Table 8. shows that, while social security spending has been increasing since the 1960s as a proportion of the national income, it is not larger in relation to all social service spending than it was then. More important, it is not much larger than it was in the 1980s and even in the 1970s. Given that the national income has almost doubled in real terms since the early 1970s, we should be able to afford much more and not just a little more for social provision without regarding it as a burden which has to be reduced.

Table 8
Social Security spending as % of UK National Income, 1948-1995

Year	National Income £s billions (1990 prices)	Total	Government Spending % of GDP All Social	Social Sec.
1948	188	40	19.0	10.1*
1958	240	41	18.0	7.2
1968	335	52	26.5	11
1978	421	51	25.8	11.6
1984	451	52	28	13.8
1995	590	51	30	14.2

Notes: * 1948 social security figure includes food subsidies. 'Social Sec.' excludes housing payment throughout
'All Social' includes education, health and housing as well as social security
Sources: *Annual Abstract of Statistics*, 1997: Tables 3.1 and 3.2 *National Income & Expenditure Blue Books*, 1954 and 1968 and *Economic Trends*, April 1979 and *Annual Supplement* 1997

CHAPTER 8

European Comparisons

If there seems to be no recent rising trend in UK Government social security spending to be detected, it might be that spending in Britain has been moving ahead of that in continental countries, and that this is the cause of Mr Blair's concern to achieve savings. There are, of course, some big differences in the size and wealth and in the economic structures of the several European countries, even among those already in the European Union. Populations vary from Germany's 81 millions and the UK's 59 millions to Luxemburg's half million and Ireland's 3.5 million. National incomes per head range almost as widely, from Switzerland and Norway's US$40,000 a year, outside the European Union, to Greece and Portugal's US$9000 inside the Union. The range is not so wide if incomes are measured in purchasing power parities instead of being translated into dollars according to exchange rates, but Switzerland still comes out at three times the level of Portugal and Greece. (Annexe Table A.1)

European countries' economies have been growing at different rates. While Sweden, Finland and even Germany have had negative 'growth' rates in the last decade, Ireland, Spain and Portugal have been catching up with much higher growth rates than the average, but this cannot be said of poor little Greece. As for the UK, it will surprise many to know that at the end of years of 'growth' the UK comes very near the bottom of the pile, in the European Union only above Ireland, Spain, Portugal and Greece in income however measured. What distinguishes the UK is the yawning gap between the rich and the poor. No other country has the poorest 20 per cent of its people with less than 5 per cent of the incomes and only Switzerland as well as the UK has the richest 20 per cent with over 44 per cent. (For all these figures see Annexe Table A.1)

Variations in the proportion of national incomes spent by governments are also very wide, and there has been some convergence here too. But the UK has been stuck in a position near to the bottom – today with only Luxemburg and Ireland having lower proportions. (Annexe Table A.2) There has been a rising trend in government spending on average throughout Europe, but two governments – Belgium and the Netherlands as well as the UK – have cut their spending proportion since 1980. So the UK government spending spree that Mr Blair is seeking to cut back as quickly as possible seems not to

Table 9
General Government Spending, 1970, 1980 1992-95 and 1997
European Countries in order of total spend per GDP, 1997

| Country | Public Expenditure as % pof GDP | | | Shares of Central Govt. Spending % | | | | | |
| | | | | Social Security | | Health | | Education | |
	1970	1980	1997	1980	1992/5	1980	1992/5	1980	1992/5
Sweden	43.2	61.6	66.9	46.4	48.2	2.0	0.2	10.5	5.0
Denmark	42.0	54.8	58.2	41.2	39.9	1.4	1.1	10.0	10.6
Norway	..	..	..	33.5	39.5	10.3	10.2	8.5	9.7
Finland	30.5	39.4	56.5	26.0	45.6	11.2	11.2	14.5	11.3
France	38.1	46.6	53.5	43.9	45.0	14.7	15.5	8.3	7.0
Belgium	41.2	57.4	53.0	41.6	..	1.7	..	14.4	..
Austria	39.1	48.8	51.7	45.1	45.8	13.2	13.2	9.6	..
Italy	32.4	42.4	51.0	31.4	..	10.8	..	9.1	..
Netherlands	41.8	56.7	50.1	37.0	37.2	11.7	14.2	12.5	10.1
EUR 11	37.0	46.6	49.4	..	..	..	..	..	..
Germany	38.5	48.0	48.9	49.5	..	19.2	16.8	0.8	0.8
Greece	..	27.3	44.9	30.6	13.4	10.5	7.4	9.6	8.5
Portugal	20.2	..	44.3	24.6	..	10.4	..	10.3	..
Spain	21.6	32.9	43.5	59.0	39.0	0.6	6.2	7.7	4.4
UK	37.3	43.2	41.3	28.3	29.6	13.2	14.0	2.2	3.3
Luxemburg	30.1	50.3	40.7	..	..	..	..	..	..
Ireland	35.5	47.8	35.2	..	28.2	..	14.0	..	12.8

Notes: Public Expenditure includes central and local spending, and public investment
Central government spending, e.g on Education, however, excludes local government spending. Thus UK total public spending on education in 1994 as a % of GNP was 5.4 and Germany's was 4.8%.
Social Security = social security and welfare, but not housing
Sources: 'Public Expenditure' from EC, *European Economy: Annual Economic Report for 1997*, 'Shares of Central Government Spending' from UNDP, *Human Development Report, 1997*, Table 35, p.212

exist, and to be relatively quite slight in the field of social protection. The share of the national income going to social security in the UK is, moreover, well below others except for Greece and Portugal. Perhaps, figures showing shares in national income give a false impression and the real increase of social spending has been faster in Britain. But this is not true either. Whether measured in real terms or in purchasing power parities, the UK from 1980 to 1994 retained its position just below the European average in expenditure on social protection (see Annexe, Table A.2).

Costs to Industry

Who has been feeding the Prime Minister with false information? And why? Could it be that the threats and rumours that Mr Blair says he wishes to discount are in fact being spread by his own spin doctors, that the aim is to continue the Tories' salami cuts in social provision so as to reduce employers' social costs? If so it is somewhat disingenuous for the 'road show' organisers to tell all who might think of joining that those business sponsors who are likely to gain from the reforms will not be welcome. In fact, all employers can expect to gain at the expense of labour. So what is the actual evidence of the comparative taxes and social contributions and comparative social costs which British industry bears compared with potential competitors?

Once again the story is the same. The UK lies in 13th place out of 20 in the list of countries ranked in order of taxes and social security contributions as a percentage of national income. Of the European countries, only Switzerland, Spain and Portugal come below the UK, joined here by the USA and Japan from outside Europe. Taxes on corporate profits made in the UK are equivalent to the European average and even somewhat below that of the USA and Japan. (See Annexe Table A.3) But social security contributions paid by employers in the UK, as a proportion of national income, are absolutely the lowest in Europe and less than those paid in the USA and Japan. (Annexe, Table A.4) And the difference is not slight: the European average is nearly three times what UK employers pay. Moreover, unit labour costs have been cut back further in real terms in the 1990s in the UK than anywhere else in Europe except in Italy and Finland. (Annexe Table A.5)

What is more important for the argument about the costs of social security is that, at the last time these were compared, in 1988, the UK had the lowest proportion of indirect costs in total industry labour costs of any of the then twelve members of the European Community. (Annexe Tables A.6 & 7) Indirect costs comprise statutory and non-statutory social security, vocational training and other services paid for by the employer. Just to add to this bonanza for employers in the UK, workers put in longer hours of work in the UK than those worked anywhere else in the European Union – 32 per cent working over 44 hours a week and 20 per cent over 48 hours, compared with a European average of 15 per cent and 8 per cent respectively. (Annexe Table A.8) The UK was, moreover, the only country where working hours were lengthened in the period recorded by Eurostat studies, between 1987 and 1991, making it the sweatshop of Europe, as Jacques Santer once implied.

Benefit and the Incentive to Work

How can one prove that it is lack of jobs rather than the attractions of welfare provision that determines the level of unemployment in any country or region? There is no doubt, of course, about the correlation of lack of economic activity with the provision of income support. Of 36 English and Welsh districts, in 1993, with more than 20 per cent of households receiving income support, all but eight had lower than average economic activity rates and some of them very much lower. The eight that were above the average were only just above, and were not concentrated in any particular region – Hastings, Merthyr Tydfil, Lambeth for example (Annexe Table A.9). Similarly, if we look at the European figures, there is no doubt also that social protection spending has risen as unemployment has risen since 1980.

Apart from these two phenomena moving together, there appears to be no other correlation between levels of unemployment and social spending among European countries. High social spending does not necessarily go with high unemployment. Indeed, taking the three years separately, 1980, 1990 and 1994: in 1980 and 1990 the countries with highest social protection – Finland, Germany, Luxemburg – had the lowest unemployment. (Annexe Table A.10) Only in 1994 does high unemployment go with high social protection, and the argument that high spending on social protection followed upon high unemployment, rather than the other way round, is strongly indicated by all the other reasons that are known for the rise in Scandinavian and German unemployment after 1990. In particular, there was the collapse of the Soviet market and the reunification of Germany.

Payments to the unemployed may take up as much as one tenth of all expenditure on social protection, when unemployment is high, and thus have a major influence on the size of the overall social security budget. The rising trend of unemployment throughout Europe has probably accounted largely for rising social security expenditure. The other reason for this rise is the same as in the UK, the increase in the number of old people in the population – in the European Union as a whole from 15 per cent in 1960, to nearly 18 per cent in 1980 and over 20 per cent today. The proportion of persons of pensionable age in the UK has moved roughly in line with that elsewhere. Pensions everywhere in Europe moved ahead faster than national incomes after 1980, and this is largely the result of the spread of supplementary voluntary schemes, which amounted by 1993 to an additional 10 per cent on average on top of the basic pension. The UK and Ireland are distinguished, however, by the very large share of the pension accounted for by such supplementary, i.e. private, schemes – over one third in the case of the UK (Annexe Table A.11), something the authors of the DSS Focus file celebrate so enthusiastically.

Invalidity and sickness benefits in most European countries take the next largest proportion of social protection after old age pensions. (Annexe Table A.12) It is the same in the UK as elsewhere. There is a suggestion in Mr Blair's *Times* article, confirmed in the Government's aim to cut back on invalidity benefit, that sickness and invalidity claims are sometimes fraudulent. They have certainly been rising in the UK, but they have not been rising much faster than national income and somewhat less rapidly in relation to national income than has been the experience in most European countries.

If only state pension provision is compared, the UK comes below even the USA and Japan at 5 per cent of national income spent in 1994, according to an article in the National Institute *Economic Review*, and that compares with over 12 per cent in France, Germany, Italy and Sweden.

What about Fraud?

Mr Blair refers to an estimate of between £4 and £5 billions of benefit fraud each year. But, in response, Professor Townsend quotes Baroness

Table 10
Social protection benefits by function, 1980 and 1994
European Countries ranked in order of total benefits, 1994

Country	Old Age (%) 1980	1994	Employment (%) 1980	1994	Sickness (%) 1980	1994	Family (%) 1980	1994
Denmark	36	38	11	16	36	28	11	8
Luxemburg	48	47	0	3	42	40	13	9
Germany	..	42	..	8	..	39	..	3
France	43	43	5	8	36	35	12	9
Netherlands	32	37	8	11	51	46	10	4
Belgium	41	44	12	11	35	35	11	8
UK	42	42	11	12	34	32	15	10
Italy	58	63	2	2	35	30	7	3
Ireland	31	27	9	12	44	38	12	13
Spain	42	44	16	18	36	35	3	2
Portugal	40	40	3	6	47	49	9	4
Greece	67	68	2	2	27	24	1	1

Notes: Columns do not necessarily add up to 100, because for some countries there are other functions not shown on the Table
'Old Age' includes 'Survivors'
'Employment' includes employment promotion and unemployment benefits
'Sickness' includes invalidity and occupational accidents
'Family' includes maternity benefit
Sources: EUROSTAT, Social Protection Expenditure and Receipts, 1980-1994, Luxemburg, 1996, Table B.6, pp.28-29

Hollis, in charge of the Government's 'Benefit Integrity Project', stating that they had not turned up any evidence of fraud affecting disability benefit. Mr Blair claims that more is spent on 'disability and incapacity benefits than . . . on the entire school system in the UK'. According to the Focus file 04, expenditure on disability and incapacity benefits rose to about £12 billion in 1995, which was almost exactly the same as was spent on schools. Thanks to the Tory Government's £3 billion proposed cuts in allowances in that year, which the DSS authors of the file euphemistically refer to as 'the changes in April 1995', expenditure will fall back in future. The fact is, however, that while the schools population has been falling, even between 1981 and 1994 from 9.1 million to 8.2 million, the numbers drawing invalidity pensions had almost doubled – from one million to two million (Annexe Table A.12) And, as Professor Townsend has pointed out, providing for school children's needs requires only a small part of the income of their families compared with the needs of the disabled. Spending on education should be increased – all are agreed on that – but should those with a disablity and incapacity be penalised? They are among many who are deprived of educational opportunity through lack of funding.

The UK is one of several countries in the European Union with slightly above the average proportion of over 60s in the population. But the increase of 90 per cent in numbers drawing invalidity allowances and disablement pensions in the UK over the years 1980 to 1992 was not a larger percentage increase than was shown in Germany, Spain and Greece, although in France and Belgium and Portugal the increase was only around 30 per cent, and in Italy the increase in disablement allowances paid seems to have cancelled out a reduction in invalidity pensions. (Annexe A.12).

What is most striking in the Eurostat reports for 1992-3 on Social Protection (Figs 3 & 4) is that, whereas the estimates of the population of disabled persons show the UK having about the average proportion of the total population with a disablement, they show that it has only half the average proportion receiving financial aid linked to a disability. Once more the UK is down with Spain and Greece, at the bottom of

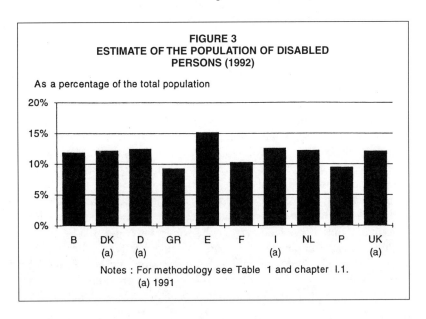

FIGURE 3
ESTIMATE OF THE POPULATION OF DISABLED
PERSONS (1992)

As a percentage of the total population

Notes : For methodology see Table 1 and chapter I.1.
(a) 1991

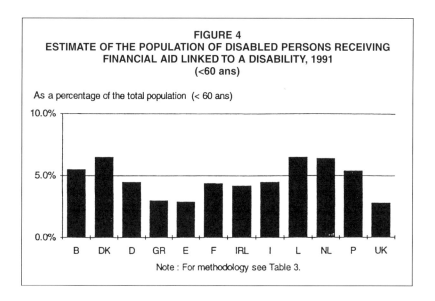

FIGURE 4
ESTIMATE OF THE POPULATION OF DISABLED PERSONS RECEIVING
FINANCIAL AID LINKED TO A DISABILITY, 1991
(<60 ans)

As a percentage of the total population (< 60 ans)

Note : For methodology see Table 3.

the league table. And since that time the cuts in allowances made by the Tory Government have come into force, including the phasing out of the earnings related incapacity benefit, for which recipients had been making their contributions over many years.

In all countries, of course, those drawing war pensions have declined in numbers as old soldiers and their widows have died, but these are listed separately from disablement and invalidity. If there is fraud, as Mr Blair suspects, in the rapid increase in disability claims in the UK, then he must be claiming that it is going on also in Germany, Spain and Greece and to a lesser extent in other EU states, where numbers of claimants have been rising rapidly. And, indeed, the proportion of national income paid out in 1994 in UK sickness and invalidity benefits was below that in other countries in the European Union, except for Greece. Denmark and Italy also had lower figures, but these are accounted for by enhanced pension provision in those countries (Table 10 above). The sharp rise in the UK in payments for sickness and disability in the years from 1991, up to the peak in 1996, when the new regulations came into force, (Focus file 04, p.7) might have been enough to make up for the UK's poor showing earlier but this must be doubted as the gap was so wide (Fig. 3); and the cuts had begun to bite in 1996

93

according to the DSS file.

Fraud is by its very nature hard to pin down but the evidence of Baroness Hollis quoted earlier was reassuring. The evidence on the ground concerning the results of the last Government's cut backs, now perpetuated by New Labour, suggests that much injustice is being done. Invalidity and sickness are determined by medical examination and rules can unfortunately be adjusted to meet the stringency of financial requirements. There is much evidence that men made redundant from industrial closures, and particularly from pit closures, have qualified for sickness benefit. Some may well have been 'carried' by their mates after injuries in their old jobs, but would not find a new job easily. Many will have tried and failed to find new work and applied for the higher rate of sickness benefit because of the absolute absence of alternative job creation in areas of industrial decline. This situation has been fully documented by the Coalfield Communities Campaign and reported in Ken Coates, MEP, and Michael Barratt Brown, *Community under Attack: The Struggle for Survival in the Coalfield Communities of Britain* (Spokesman, 1997).

It would seem to be a strange way to tackle fraud to reduce the levels of social security payment. Most people faced by such reductions would seek to do everything possible to maximise their benefits. The campaign against fraud also consorts ill with Mr Blair's aim to get more money to those in need who do not now claim the income support to which they are entitled. More means testing and more inspectors will hardly encourage those who are too frightened or too ignorant to claim what is owing to them. At the root of all fraud must lie the lack of work and opportunities for work at a living wage. Create the jobs and the problem solves itself, and, as Professor Townsend has insisted, 'benefit fraud when properly investigated turns out to be much smaller than claimed, and is far smaller in total value than tax evasion and tax fraud.'

Family allowances form another benefit under attack from the salami chopper. Payments in the UK under this heading are only just above the average in value and in relation to national income, when compared with others in the European Union, but there is one big difference in the conditions for eligibility. In the UK a much larger proportion is subject to a means test than is normal elsewhere, except in Ireland. Moreover, while basic schemes have gone down in real value in the UK, down rather more than the average for the rest of the

EU, the means tested proportion has risen correspondingly faster. According to the Focus files, the proportion of benefits that are means tested doubled between 1979/80 and 1995/6 from 16 per cent to 35 per cent. By contrast in Denmark and Luxemburg family benefit is more than twice what it is in the UK, and in France and Germany 50 per cent larger, and, except in Germany, almost all without means testing (Annexe Table 13).

It was argued at the beginning, with authoritative support, that far from cutting child benefit the Government should greatly increase its value. This would do more than anything else to encourage women (and men too) to look for work, even at low wages, if they are not already doing so, but also provide for women who feel that they need to stay with their young children. Studies that have been made show that there is very little evidence of skiving, whatever the tabloid press may say. The Employment Services' 1992 Report, *Employment in Britain*, described a survey of a sample 1000 unemployed and 3000 employed people and found that commitment to work (defined as 'would work even if there was no financial necessity') was very high. It was higher among unemployed people (76 per cent) than among those in employment (68 per cent). Similar results were found in surveys made in Coalfield areas (see *Community under Attack*, Coates and Barratt Brown, Spokesman 1997).

What Price Maternity?

Maternity benefit in the UK has attracted the most criticism from the new Minister for Social Security, a mother herself. This benefit is not means tested, so that the criticism is presumably on the grounds of Mr Blair's criterion of 'spending the tax-payers' money wisely'. Since the cash benefit is paid on the basis of lost salary, one mother with an income of over £1 million was said to have been paid £20,000 in maternity benefit. The story was carefully supplied to the Murdoch press, which lapped it up as an example of the need for 'reform'. But it should surely never have been agreed that the employer should be refunded by the state for such employment costs.

In fact, as has already been emphasised, the reform needed would primarily be in the tax system, which fails to tax such grotesque incomes at higher rates, following the Tory Government's abolition of the higher rate bands, which New Labour apparently is not willing to restore. In any case the average cash benefit of all kinds for a non-retired household in the top 20 per cent of UK households is only £800 a year to add to an average original income of over £40,000 (see Table 4 above). In the over £1 million a year income band, cash benefits of a few hundred pounds would not appear very large, and the number of such incomes among women must be very small. In fact, the Labour Research Department failed to find any such example, but did find that women earning over £30,000 a year only accounted for 5 per cent of the actual maternity payments.

There has been some talk of an affluence test, but this would not only be difficult to administer, but would be quite without effect until a serious effort is made to deal with all those tax dodges which Mr Gordon Brown, before he came to power, said he was going to stop. It also creates a difficult problem that already faces those who wish once more to treat partners as single tax units for tax credit schemes and thus end the woman's much treasured and only newly found financial independence.

In fact, maternity benefits as a proportion of national incomes have been declining in most European countries, but not in the UK. While the UK is among the higher spenders in Europe on maternity benefit, a far smaller proportion of this is paid in cash in the UK and a much larger proportion on hospital and other medical services than in other countries (Annexe Table A.14). Of course, European countries have different ways of providing hospital and othe medical services, which accounts for the wide variation in cash payments.

Given that fertility rates have gone down very rapidly in Europe in the last 30 years – from 2.61 in 1960 to 1.48 in 1992 on average among the EUR 12 and from 2.72 to 1.79 in the UK – further reductions in maternity benefits must be regarded as inadvisable. Any rate below 2.0 per female member of the population naturally implies a declining population. Some might prefer this, but it carries the implication of an ever smaller population of young people to work for an ever larger population of old people. It looks like playing to the gallery of tabloid press readers rather than serious policy making for the Government to be fussing about putting curbs on universal maternity benefit.

CHAPTER 9

What Should be Reformed

Mr Blair in his *Times* article listed the main changes in our society to which, he believed, the welfare state must adapt: most people changing jobs at least five or six times in their career, more women at work, people living longer, up to 30 years after retirement, more marriages ending in divorce. There is no doubt about the truth of all of these assumptions except the first one, which we can look at in a footnote (p.102 below).

But Mr Blair has drawn the wrong conclusions, which we can discuss at the end, and he has missed out the most important changes as they affect the provision of welfare. The first is the change in the balance in our lives of paid work and leisure. The second is the crumbling framework of the nation state which has to support the welfare state. We are already beginning to see the reduction in the hours and years of paid work and the corresponding increase in the time devoted to what we call leisure activities, including studying. This process is certain to continue, in spite of the long hours that those who have paid work spend at work. Many others find themselves without work or facing early retirement. Both are at present involuntary. Both are feared and abhorred. It is not so much the loss of income but the loss of work-mates and of an abiding interest in life.

Work and Leisure

Most leisure activities require money – for transport, for travel, for tools and equipment to pursue the arts, sports, gardening and other DIY activities. Moreover, they are only easily affordable with public provision – of transport, sports facilities, allotments, museums, galleries and concert halls. The individualistic view of welfare which sees individuals living on their own savings to follow their own pursuits irrespective of others is a narrow one; and Mr Blair's occasional appeal to a communitarian rhetoric finds a wide response. But there must be substance in the promise. There can be no community without some shared finance and shared services which are universal and not divisive and exclusive. Much of this can be supplied by voluntary effort, but it needs a foundation of public provision. And this should be part of the meaning of welfare. Where in the UK we talk about redistributive taxation, on the continent they speak of solidarity taxes.

All the pressure to get people off welfare and into work is quite misconceived, if machines are going to take over more and more of the labour we have now to supply to maintain our livelihood. The evidence supplied by expert opinion is that a working life of 1000 hours a year is likely within two or three decades. Already the average in Germany is 1500 compared with 1900 in the UK. The concern with finding paid work for all who want it is not misplaced, but the single minded concentration on work for work's sake and for some supposed competitive advantage is mistaken. The UK has the longest average hours of work of any European country. A tax framework that assists the sharing of work is what is required, not pressure to get everyone into work regardless.

The Limits of the Nation State

The weakening of the nation state creates more serious problems for the future of welfare than any of the other changes. Increasing globalisation of capital accumulation has not destroyed the powers of the nation state, but it has put all but the most powerful states at the mercy of the giant transnational companies which dominate the world's economy. To attract the investment of these companies, each separate state enters a Dutch auction competing to offer the cheapest labour and the least regulated environment. Mr Blair has nailed his colours to the mast in the matter of deregulation. Britain is going to compete, not to have the best social protection, but the lowest taxes for the employer. As we have seen (Annexe Table A.4) this was already achieved by a Tory Government in 1994. New Labour proposes to build on that, or rather to dismantle social protection still further.

There is a real problem here. So long as each nation seeks to manage its own welfare state, capitalist competition will tend to drive down labour costs. About a quarter of these are indirect (Annexe Table A.6). These are charges for social security and vocational training etc. The threat of unbridled competition to such social protection led to the inclusion of a Social Chapter in the Maastricht Treaty, which a Tory government opted out of and New Labour seems reluctant to accept in full. International agreement on social protection is the only answer to a bidding down everywhere of state provision.

A common European commitment to minimum levels of provision is not only imperative for social cohesion, but, as Stuart Holland has for long insisted, it is an economic imperative (Stuart Holland, *The European Imperative*, Spokesman, 1993). The reason for this lies in the reduced purchasing power of an increasingly unequal economy. High rates of growth and high levels of employment are associated everywhere, according to the UNDP *Human Development Reports*, with greater equality of incomes. The United States is the great exception. Actual unemployment in the US is masked by the massive prison population, but, more generally, the exception depends on the hegemonic economic and military power which allows the United States economy to draw in the loans and investment of the whole world.

Welfare and Social Change

What was the purpose of Mr Blair's list of changes in the way we live and work, especially in relation to women, when he asks us to agree to the reform of the welfare state? More women at work means less reliance on a man's wage and pension rights. This should be a good thing, but most of the new employment of women is part-time and much of it carries no requirement on the employer (or employee) to contribute to National Insurance – or any other insurance. Mr Blair says nothing about making this requirement universal, although non-contribution is doubtfully legal under the European Social Charter. More divorces strengthens the case for women to have their own pension rights and to have more and not less support as single parents. The attempt to move single mothers from welfare to work by reducing their benefit fails to take account not only of the absence of jobs and of adequate day care provision, but of the lack of insurance cover for women working part-time. Given the very low general level of their wages, there is little or no possibility that they might build up their own insurances.

In this matter as well as in the larger question of the state pension, the view of the new government seems to be that individuals -- men and women – should now make their own individual private insurance arrangements against unemployment, sickness and old age. We are back to the Nineteenth Century with a vengeance. The fact that all incomes are higher now than then does not help the poor, for whom modern living in apartments and estates implies central heating, refrigerators, washing machines, packaged food and transport to the nearest shop, whose price is set by the average buyers and not by the poorer ones. Higher inomes, as we observed earlier, should imply more rather than less ability to pay taxes to ensure a proper health service and education system for all and the possibility of income redistribution to reduce inequalities.

The assumption by Mr Blair of frequent job changes is designed to support the idea of a personalised insurance system, which the individual worker can carry with him or her from job to job.

Requiring all employers to contribute to such schemes for part-time as well as full-time workers at appropriate rates would be a big step forward, but such schemes carry with them no element of redistribution by the Government. By contrast, as we have had it under the National Insurance scheme, payments are made progressively up to a point according to levels of earnings, but every one receives the same in benefits and in health and education. Where the scheme failed was that the cut-off point left the richest 20 per cent paying no more than those below them. Had they done so, the crisis of underfunding of the state pension need not have occurred. So we were assured by the leading expert on pensions, Professor Peter Townsend, in the pamphlet which he wrote jointly with Barbara Castle and in the Socialist Renewal pamphlet, *New Directions for Pensions*, written with Alan Walker (Spokesman, 1995).

The Case for the State Pension

In their pamphlet, Peter Townsend and Alan Walker foresaw that

'Labour's policy on pensions will set the scene for its entire social and economic policy for five years. Its pension policy will be seen widely as a key indicator of Labour's will to change the unstable, divided and more widely impoverished society inherited from 16 years of Conservative free market policies.'

They put forward six arguments in favour of restoring the universal state pension plus SERPS rather than supporting further the increased role of occupational and private pensions with a safety net of a minimum state guarantee, which would inevitably be means tested. The arguments were first that means tested income support failed to be claimed by one third of eligible pensioners. These are the very people who Mr Blair says the welfare system is failing. So it is, but it is means testing, not the basic pension, they are refusing. Secondly occupational, private or personal pensions are of little or no use to those, especially women, without full-time labour market careers. Thirdly, only a universal public provision can give economic security in an increasingly flexible and insecure labour market (indeed Townsend and Walker argue that a basic pension will actually assist flexibility). Fourthly, a universal state pension minimises inequalities between older men and women. Fifthly, it is the cheapest form of pension to administer – 1p in the £, compared with 11p on means tested income support and 25p or more on private pensions, with all the possibilities we have seen of mis-selling and other abuse. Finally, its very universality and equitable basis enhances social cohesion and solidarity between the generations.

The cost of increasing the basic pension in line with earnings was calculated by Townsend and Walker at 0.4 per cent of annual GDP and for the restoration of SERPS a further 0.8 per cent of GDP. According to John Hills in a Joseph Rowntree Foundation Inquiry, the combined costs of these two over the next 50 years would come to less than a quarter of the cost of the 1992-5 recession. They would, moreover, be offset by reductions in the need for means-tested income support and other contingent benefits. The extra money would have to be found from raising the ceiling for National Insurance Contributions, raising the rate for highest salary earners, increasing the rate for employers of large numbers of employees, and limiting subsidies in the private sector while tightening up on tax avoidance. It will be impossible, Townsend and Walker believe, to develop a viable pensions policy without European policy collaboration. But that does not mean downgrading the provision in the rest of Europe to the mean levels of the UK. They quote as an example to emulate the Danish Social Pension. This provides the sole pension for four fifths of Danish pensioners, and at a level of disposable income after housing costs that is equal to 77 per cent of the average income of the whole population.

---

* The one exception in Mr Blair's statement about the changes affecting welfare provision is the one about the increase in job instability. The International Labour Office in the chapter entitled 'Is Full Employment Passé?' of its 1996/7 Report quoted a study of job stability by K. Swinnerton and H. Wial in the *Industrial and Labour Relations Review* for January 1995. This reached the following conclusions from studies of data in the United States and in the UK:

'The proportion of workers whose jobs will ultimately last zero to three years decreased slightly from 31.8 per cent in the 1979-83 period to 30.9 per cent in the 1987-91 period. The proportion of those who will keep the same job for four to seven years increased from 14 per cent to 15 per cent over the same period, while the proportion of those staying in their job more than eight years remained stable at 54.1 per cent . . .' Thus they believe that 'the data do not suggest that the entire 1979-91 period was a time of increasing job instability'.

Periods of boom and slump must affect stability, but over a longer period, the ILO's own studies suggested that in France and Germany around 60 per cent of male wage workers can expect to keep their jobs more than 15 years. The proportions are only somewhat lower in the USA and Canada, where we are told flexibility of employment is general. The ILO does not see increased instability occurring in the UK, although there is evidence of this in Spain.

CHAPTER 10

Towards a New Manifesto

The old state pension was part of the universal welfare system devised by William Beveridge in 1942 and introduced by the 1945 Labour Government. Mr Blair says that New Labour's principles are still the same as Beveridge's, but they cannot be the same if he moves the welfare system from a universal system to a fall-back system of minimum guaranteed state benefits. We have seen that private pension arrangements have begun to supply an increasing part of the average pension in the UK, over a third by 1993. Increasing numbers of people who can afford it, take out medical insurance. The numbers of children being educated in Britain at private schools does not decline, indicating a rise in the proportion outside the state system. Payment of fees is now introduced for higher education with a personal loan system for maintenance in place of the old grant system.

Of course, Mr Blair is right to identify the changing structure of family life as affecting all welfare provision. The Beveridge system was based on the assumption that the man's wage supplied the contributions to ensure protection for wife and family in the event of sickness, unemployment and old age. The facts Mr Blair attests: that most women now work, though not necessarily, as we have seen, being covered by National Insurance; that the nuclear family is almost the exception and not the rule; and above all that women have won much greater independence, means that this aspect of the system needs to be changed. Individuals and not families need to be insured and guaranteed basic rights of social protection in a society where the overwhelming majority of both men and women can only get a living by selling their labour to a private employer.

The conclusion from all this, however, does not follow that it should be left to the individual to make his or her own best bargain and best arrangements. With the support of strong trade unions that might be more acceptable, but Mr Blair does not appear to be enamoured of strong trade unions, and the unions share with the nation state the weaknesses of being open to division and conquest by the international employing companies. The nation state, or the wider association of states today, still carries the responsibility to ensure the basic civil rights of all citizens and not just minimum rights for those who are excluded from the main stream of national life.

Abandoning universality in welfare must imply means testing and a steady differentiation in the services supplied. It can only mean a perpetuation of the inequalities that have grown under past Tory governments to make the UK the most inegalitarian of all the states of Western Europe through both cutting benefits and undermining wage levels with the abolition of the Wages Councils. But inequality means also persisting poverty. And poverty, as the UNDP Human Development studies reveal, is associated with a general lowering of human development. After Ireland and Spain, the UK has the largest proportion of its population in poverty of all Western European countries. From being third in rank in West Europe according to the UNDP's Human Development Index in 1960, it has fallen to ninth place, and in the world league from fifth to fifteenth (Table 11).

Yes Mr Blair we need reform to meet people's changing work styles, but not if that means dismantling what still exists of the social insurance system and keeping the iniquitous taxation arrangements.

Reform of the welfare state requires the most comprehensive official examination of the costs and benefits of the present system, not selective quotations from the statistics to justify a programme of cuts, laced with exhortations to self-improvement. Unofficially, this has already been done in John Hills report on Income and Wealth for the Joseph Rowntree Foundation in 1995. If it needs to be updated, the Department of Social Security and the Inland Revenue will have all the figures which are required to find out who pays and who gains, who could pay more and who should receive more. Before any further cuts are made, we need to know all the facts. But we need also to have an open discussion involving independent experts with the power to reveal all the facts in the UK and in other countries, especially those in the European Union, and with the authority to publish them, so that the

Table 11
Human Development Index (HDI) and Poverty, 1960, 1980 and 1994
European Countries in HDI order 1994

Country	Human Development Index (maximum = 1.000)			Population in Poverty % under $14 a day
	1960	*1980*	*1994*	*1989-94*
France	0.853	0.895	0.946	12
Norway	0.865	0.901	0.943	3
Netherlands	0.855	0.888	0.940	14
Finland	0.811	0.880	0.940	4
Sweden	0.867	0.899	0.936	5
Spain	0.636	0.851	0.934	21
Austria	0.797	0.880	0.932	. .
Belgiuim	0.826	0.873	0.932	12
UK	0.857	0.892	0.931	13
Switzerland	0.853	0.897	0.930	. .
Ireland	0.710	0.862	0.929	37
Denmark	0.857	0.888	0.927	8
Germany	0.841	0.881	0.924	12
Greece	0.573	0.839	0.923	. .
Italy	0.755	0.857	0.921	2
Luxemburg	0.826	0.869	0.899	4
Portugal	0.460	0.736	0.890	. .

Notes: HDI is a composite index composed of three variables: life expectancy, educational attainment (adult literacy and combined primary, secondary and tertiary enrolment) and real GDP per capita in (in PPP$)
Sources: UNDP *Human Development Report, 1997,* Annexe Table A.2.1 and p. 53 and Table 5, p. 158

people of this country can discover what has been done to them and what will be done, unless the direction of welfare provision in Britain is radically changed to reduce inequalities in society instead of perpetuating them.

A Labour Movement

The idea of a Labour Movement in Britain is a very old one. It reflects the historic links between the trade unions and the Labour Party. It appears that these links are finally to be severed by New Labour. As this Manifesto is being written, the TUC General Council has returned from a meeting with the Prime Minister in Downing Street and the news is that Mr Blair will not provide the promised recognition in law for trade unions in establishments where a 'majority among the relevant workforce' votes for it. Today no more than 20% of private sector employees belong to a union and collective bargaining covers less than 50% of the workforce. It is, as John Monks, the TUC General Secretary said, 'a defining moment'. After almost two decades of Conservative Government onslaught on their rights and privileges, the unions expected support from a New Labour government. It seems that they are not to get it.

The implications of this decision are enormous. The protection of men and women under the social security system, when they are out of work through sickness, unemployment or old age, which has been the subject of this Manifesto, cannot be separated from the protection that workers look to from their unions when they are in work. Some unions have been criticised for their lack of concern for the unemployed and the retired, but they have always assumed that this was the responsibility of the political wing of the Movement. Without that, the position of labour in Britain in relation to the power of capital is severely weakened. What has been done to working people in two decades in the destruction of great industries without measures to create new employment and in the dismantling of the welfare state has amounted to a massive act of violence against whole communities, leaving in its wake a tide of bitterness and despair.

The virtual annihilation of the Tory Party in Labour's electoral victory a year ago was a collective act of revenge and an expression of hope and of faith that change was possible. It seems that that hope and that faith are to be betrayed. It is not just that the government of New Labour is neutral between capital and labour. Mr Blair before the election promised no favours for either. In the event it is the owners and managers of capital who have received the favours. Big business men, both industrialists and bankers, have been brought in by the Government to represent it in key positions, as in the negotiations with the European Union, and to head up QUANGOs and important inquiries into future policy. These include most particularly the review of taxes and benefits for the Chancellor by Sir Mark Turner of Barclays Bank. The traditional conservatism of the Treasury concerning all extensions of public spending and taxation has been constantly reinforced by the pressure of Big Business leaders including the moguls of the media.

The Philosophy of New Labour in a Changing World

The Independent Labour Network has maintained from the beginning that New Labour is not simply following where the last Conservative Government led, in dismantling the welfare state and destroying trade union power, but has its own particular philosophical position. New Labour spokesmen and women deny that the old battles of capital and labour are any longer relevant. They have returned to revive a still older struggle, that between the individual and the state. This is in response to three major changes in social relations in the last decades. The first is that a sizeable minority of the population, without inherited ownership of land or capital, have achieved through their intellectual, artistic or athletic skills a degree of financial independence that makes them unresponsive to traditional collective organisation. A new spirit of individualism has begun to spread through society, stimulated by the media of press and television which reflect the advertising power of the giant manufacturers and retailers of consumer goods and services. This individualism has found its own expression in the burgeoning informal economy and increasing lawlessness where the great industrial communities of the past have been destroyed.

The second change in social relations, which has greatly reinforced the first, is the rightful demand of women for economic and legal independence. The strongest case against the old welfare system is that it was based upon the male earner's income and social insurance contributions to protect his wife and family. After marriage a woman's earnings were regarded as marginal, the wife of an unemployed or sick working man was assumed to be dependent, in old age the woman shared the man's pension – at a lower rate for a couple than for two individuals. When Harriet Harman cries out against such a system, she carries the women with her. The failure of the new intake of women into the House of Commons to vote against the cut in the lone parents' benefit was not just done from cowardice or concern to protect a woman minister, but from a visceral rejection by professional women of a system that had for so long treated them as dependents. This flaw does not necessarily, however, put into question the whole system of social insurance, as we have demonstrated earlier.

The third reason for the abandonment of the collectivism of the welfare state is that the powers of the nation state, which was its foundation, have become suborned almost everywhere to the demands of the giant international accumulations of capital. Mr Blair is right to recognise that small to medium sized states have little power today to maintain tax regimes that are unacceptable to the great transnational companies. They will simply transfer their investments and their profits elsewhere to places where conditions are more favourable for their capital accumulation. This is not entirely a new phenomenon, but the new information technology has made the globalisation of production as well as of finance much more all embracing than before.

The Alternatives: Competition or Cooperation

In these new circumstances, there are two alternatives for a medium sized state like the United Kingdom. The first is that chosen by Mr Blair. That is to seek to make the local economy as competitive in world markets as is possible by offering to transnational capital the most skilled professionals, the cheapest labour, the lowest taxes and the least regulated environment, including trade union as well as physical and ecological controls, of any competing state economy. The drive to move men and women, young and old, able and disabled, out of welfare and into work not only reduces the indirect social protection costs of labour but by increasing the supply of labour lowers its direct price in the market. Mr Blair's constant repetition of the need to be competitive embraces the whole nation but is directed at every individual. Compete or die is the message.

How far Mr Blair and his colleagues actually see what they are doing like that may be doubted, but they are driven by the logic of events, once they have rejected the alternative. Mr Blair employs a communitarian rhetoric and a Christian zeal, but his appeal is to individual self-help. He refers to his policies as following a 'third way' between the extremes of unregulated private capital and of over regulated public ownership. He is right to say that this is the old choice, but his is not the only 'third way'. Indeed his 'third way' is hard to distinguish from the way of unregulated private capital, towards which he is inevitably driven by the power of capital in global markets.

What then is the alternative which he has rejected? Is there in fact a real alternative that is based on collective action but allows to individuals the freedoms that many have come to enjoy? Or is it in the end indistinguishable from the overregulated totalitarian systems, which have collapsed everywhere? Democratic socialists have undoubtedly

MAY DAY MANIFESTO

failed to make their case and the Blairites have won by default. A powerful argument has been mounted in this Manifesto against the individualist approach to welfare provision, but the collectivist alternative may seem all too similar to what has been rejected in the past. The study of social protection in other European countries which we have made has shown that, in spite of the financial difficulties of surviving individually in a competitive global economy and of the constraints of modelling an Economic and Monetary Union in Europe to compete in that economy, the welfare state outside the UK has survived. Only in Britain has it been cut back to the level of the poorest countries of southern Europe.

That is the first answer, that the welfare state is compatible with democratic government in mixed economies. It also suggests at once the alternative to going it alone in single handed competition to win the favours of international capital. It is to cooperate with others in Europe in defending their welfare states and resisting the power of the giant international companies' attempts to divide and conquer. The opportunity to work together rather than in competition exists. Under Conservative administrations the British people have been held back from taking advantage of these opportunities, but New Labour has given some indication of ending that stance. The possibilities of working together to draw on best practice rather than running a Dutch auction of worsening labour conditions are there to be seized. Harriet Harman in her *Guardian* article of March 31st 1998 wrote of the consultations that will follow the Government's acceptance of the 'Social Chapter' and its implications for shorter working hours, parental leave and part-time working. It will simply not be acceptable for Britain to continue to force down European wages and conditions of work.

Mr Blair will soon learn, if he does not yet understand, the importance of the collective role of trade unions and of a sense of social security in maintaining the enthusiasm, indeed the very morale, of any workforce. The fact is that the dichotomy between competition and cooperation, between individualism and collectivism is never so sharp in real life as it is drawn by the ideologists. The secret of Japanese economic success hitherto has been the encouragement of competition within a powerful cooperative framework, created, developed and maintained by state institutions. Competing private companies everywhere support professional and technical insitutions for the exchange of information about new research and development. The organisation of giant companies is less and less based upon hierarchies of command and increasingly upon networking between decentralised independent profit centres. Mr Blair in extolling individual self-help knows that in every enterprise, public or private, competitiveness has to be moderated by teamwork. We noted earlier how the Green Paper on welfare reform, in the middle of a rhapsody on individual self-help, appealed for the public service ethos in the delivery of welfare.

Social Provision that is also Individual

The conflict in human thought and action between the individual and the collective, between competition and co-operation, between rational calculation and mystical faith, is as old as recorded time. But for a thousand years it was fought out between individualist secular capitalism and a universal hierarchical church. The state has been the battleground sometimes captured by the Church (not only Catholic but also Communist); increasingly in recent years by capitalism. The modern welfare state was, however, created in response to a new force in world history – that of labour, struggling against both capitalist and bureaucratic power. Collectivity did not need to be based upon mysticism but could have firm scientific foundations. It was nation states that had supported the development of capitalism and it was to the nation state that the disinherited turned for protection. Even the workers' trade unions had first to win state recognition to be effective in defending their members' jobs and conditions of work. And from recognition they had moved under Labour Party leadership to make a challenge to capitalist power.

Today this challenge has been checked. This began with an open offensive by a government of the radical Right which started dismantling the welfare state and using unemployment as a tool of monetary management. It has been continued by New Labour in a less open manner, converting the welfare state from a universal source of solidarity into a safety net for those who can prove a 'genuine need' for what are offensively called 'hand-outs', and relegating full employment to second place after the value of money.

The challenge to capital by labour is transmuted into the promise of participation, with labour as the junior partner. The Unions' power is still to be firmly circumscribed, while business is given free rein.

Working people whatever their endowment are to make their own way in the market. They will be divided and defeated if they do not find ways to unite in collective defence of the welfare state, with appropriate amendments to recognise the equality of women and the importance of part-time work; and in defence of the fundamental human right of a worthwhile occupation for all men and women.

The Independent Labour Network has argued in this Manifesto that no amount of preparation for work of young men, young mothers, long term unemployed or the disabled will be of any avail, if there are no jobs to be had at the end. The task of government has to be not only to provide advice and training and education, a service of health and protection for the disadvantaged; it must also be prepared to create employment. It is an ironic tragedy, which we have already recognised, that just when the main body of economic thought is moving back towards the conviction that full employment is a proper and possible aim of government policy, Mr Blair should be continuing to rely on the market to create jobs. Welfare into work is a splendid slogan if the work is being made available, and the work that needs to be done in our society is unbounded – in clearing up pollution, in recycling waste, in insulating houses, in creating and maintaining parks and leisure facilities, and above all in providing opportunities for lifelong learning.

All these issues crystallised in the European Appeal for Full Employment, which was launched in 1996. It attracted the support of over 600 parliamentarians, including more than 160 Members of the European Parliament, as well as hundreds of trade unions, church bodies and other non-governmental organisations concerned with social questions. The Appeal formed the basis for the first European Convention for Full Employment. This brought together nearly a thousand participants at the European Parliament in Brussels in May 1997. The second Full Employment Convention is planned to meet in Brussels in November 1998.

This Appeal (printed below) has proved capable of uniting socialists of different schools with the main green parties in Europe and other independent radicals in joint and common action. It has done this on the basis of its appreciation of the changing patterns of work in modern society, as well as the continuing humanistic recognition that full employment remains the very foundation of a free society.

Full Employment: A European Appeal

'In Europe today we live in a rich world. Yet our societies are deeply flawed. Millions of our fellow citizens seek paid work and cannot find it: many more than the 20 million officially unemployed. Many women, and many older men have given up the search. In some regions, among our young people, one in five cannot find paid work. In regions of high unemployment, up to half the young people are without employment. More than half of the unemployed have been without employment for over a year, and half of these even for two years or more. Ever more women and men are being excluded from any hope of earning their living by actively contributing to their societies' wealth. The welfare state is cut back, unable to cope with continuous unemployment. In some countries this misery has lasted for fifteen years.

We should call this exclusion from society by its right name: it is a disaster which is destroying people's lives, dissolving the social fabric in which we live and depend on one another, undermining the very foundations of democratic politics. It calls for urgent relief.

Creative work for each individual, personal participation in the production of wealth, and corresponding remuneration, are no less basic human needs than are the needs for food, clothing, and shelter. Unemployment generates insecurity and despair. Sickness frequently visits those who are unemployed, so that people may find their health undermined at the same time that they face poverty and social isolation.

Unemployment does not just happen. It is man made. Full employment can surely be achieved again, even if it is not the same kind of full employment we knew during the long post-war period in most Western European countries. Instead of guaranteeing a "family wage" to the male wage earners, leaving other necessary work to be done by women as unpaid work, full employment will now be about guaranteeing access to properly paid work to every independent member of society, thus furthering the redistribution of unpaid work in a fair and better way. And rather than relying on a continuous expansion of every kind of material production, full employment will now have to be based on careful stewardship of natural resources and decent environmental conditions. Since Western European societies are at least three times richer than they were at the birth of post-war welfare politics, we could, in fact, afford to achieve such a new kind of full employment – by supporting an ecologically sustainable recovery, by redistributing paid (and unpaid) work, as well as through private incomes and public goods.

Everywhere there is a need for public provision of shared services. No one doubts the usefulness, for example, of our caring services, or preventive health work, or of education and training. Why should we not also co-operate in restoring run-down areas, in recuperation of the natural environment, in improving housing security and energy efficiency, in developing sheltered housing for old people, or in offering better child care support, and sport and leisure centres for the young? Is there not equal benefit in support for small and medium enterprises, or for sustainable agriculture? Yet vital services are allowed to decline and decay in a destructive spiral. Public expenditure is reduced, instead of reducing public waste and tax fraud. At the same time, new technologies and methods of organisation are used to lay off ever more people, instead of offering them a role in a better network of public provision, and creating more, better qualified and better paid jobs.

Capital movements, all kinds of speculation and even production itself, are now more than ever arranged on an international, global scale. National governments have been set against each other, and trade unions and the working people of each country have been dragged into an economic war for competitive advantage. The arguments supporting this harmful process are misleading: in general, the rate of profitability in Western Europe is far above the global average, and even in countries which are at the forefront of world competition there are real alternatives to the kind of monetaristic policies currently being imposed.

The European Commission and Council of Ministers have launched various plans and proposals over the last few years to create large numbers of jobs all across the Union. But from the launch of the Delors White Paper to the Conclusions of the Essen Summit, in spite of a modest economic recovery in the meantime, the number of people in work has not risen. Throughout Western Europe, the numbers employed remain at least 16 million below what they were in 1990. At the same time, improvements in the number of women finding jobs in parts of the economy are marred by the insecurities of part-time work, and by severely exploitative low pay, while there has been a marked fall in male full-time jobs. The pattern of working time is still organised according to traditional roles for men and women, without adequately recognising the profound changes that have already taken place. Continued large increases in productivity mean that working hours overall can, and should be cut, without the reduction of the resources allocated to pay. At the same time, new fiscal policies could help safeguard earnings and income levels. Indeed, we now face the danger that unemployment and poor jobs will increase, as governments cut back their spending to meet their very restrictive interpretation of the terms of the Maastricht Treaty for a single currency. Now, in many countries, we face a combination of social cuts with the removal of social protection in the labour market. A new misery threatens: the descent into poverty of those who have been long excluded, and of those others who now endure painfully low wages, saps the confidence and strength of their neighbours, and brings fear and insecurity to large parts of Europe.

This European crisis is replicated throughout the world, and we seek allies in every continent to work out employment policies based on co-operation rather than raw competition.

There is no case for a fortress economy, either at the level of Europe, or at the levels of a nation, a region, or a family. Some have tried: the rich in some countries fortify their suburbs, carry guns and teach their children to shoot. This will not work. The only way forward is to act together, each for all, striking a "new deal" from below, between the poor and the better-off, using the instruments of public policy to advance common interests capable of stabilising broad popular alliances. At local, regional, national and European levels, we need joint and common action to create and to safeguard sufficiently well-paid jobs, and to re-distribute working time.

We have to persuade a broad majority of the people that it is better to finance socially useful and ecologically sustainable work than to subsidise unemployment. We want to press for a common European economic strategy to reduce unemployment, exclusion, and poverty on the way towards a new era of full employment. This choice involves a wide variety of public and private programmes, including a European level of borrowing and funding, and sustained efforts to reduce working time, share work, and make possible a rich programme of lifelong learning, while at the same time safeguarding the income levels of the working population.

New technologies and new management systems need fewer

workers to produce more goods and services. Labour is, in fact, saved this way. We need, however, to use this saved labour in a new sharing of paid and unpaid labour, reducing the gap between those who are overworked, and those who are excluded from society's work, as well as using some of the additional earnings for funding the creation of jobs in the environment, education, and the caring services. Voluntary bodies, churches, and trade unions have already begun to study the effect of sabbatical leave for parents, the provision of training and schooling in working time, and other relevant methods of sharing work, as well as creating humane and satisfying forms of work to replace much labour that is boring and repetitive drudgery.

This Appeal seeks to encourage all forms of action and all modes of employment which will end the disaster of unemployment. Its signatories will seek ways to come together to exchange ideas, examine experiences, and co-ordinate their work. We shall seek to encourage relevant action in the political field, so that employment takes its place at the top of the agenda. We shall also do whatever we can to influence our neighbours and communities to refuse a Europe of exclusion and mass unemployment. Europe must include all its citizens, and afford to each the space in which to develop his or her capacity for happiness and social solidarity.'

Annexe One: Statistics

Table A.1
Income Per Head, 1995, Growth. 1985-95 and Distribution, 1988
European Countries ranked in $ income order

Country	Income 1995 000 US$	Income 1995 000 PPP	Growth % 1985-95	Income shares Bottom 20%	Income shares Top 20%	Gap
Switzerland	40.6	29.5	0.2	5.2	44.6	39.4
Norway	39.6	22.1	1.7	6.2	36.7	30.5
Denmark	31.2	21.9	1.5	5.4	38.6	33.2
Germany	27.5	20.1	-0.1	7.0	40.3	32.7
Austria	26.9	21.2	1.0	. .	. .	. .
France	25.0	21.0	1.5	5.6	41.9	36.3
Belgium	24.7	21.7	2.2	7.9	36.0	28.1
Netherlands	24.0	20.0	1.9	8.2	36.9	28.7
Sweden	23.7	18.5	-0.1	8.0	36.9	28.9
Finland	20.6	17.8	-0.2	6.3	37.6	31.3
Italy	19.0	19.9	1.8	6.8	41.0	34.2
UK	18.7	19.3	1.4	4.6	44.3	39.7
Ireland	14.7	15.7	5.2	. .	. .	. .
Spain	13.6	14.5	2.6	8.3	36.6	28.3
Portugal	9.7	12.7	3.6	. .	. .	. .
Greece	8.2	11.7	1.3	. .	. .	. .

Notes: PPP = Purchasing Power Parities used instead of exchange rates for converting GDP to US$s
'Gap' in income shares is the difference between the share of the top 20% and that of the bottom 20%
Sources: World Bank, *World Development Report*, Oxford, 1997: Tables 1 and 5, pp. 215 and 223

Table A.2
Total Social Protection Expenditure Per Head, 1980, 1992, 1994
(000 ECU at 1985 prices) and 1994 at current prices and PPPs
European Countries, 1980 and 1992 in 1994 ranking

Rank	Country	1980 1985 prices	1992 1985 prices	1994	1994 current prices	1994 PPPs
1.	Denmark	3.8	5.1	5.8	8.0	6.4
2.	Luxemburg	3.0	4.6	5.2	7.3	6.6
3.	Germany	3.6	4.6	4.6	6.5	5.5
4.	France	3.0	4.3	4.5	5.9	5.5
5.	Netherlands	3.5	4.4	4.3	5.9	5.5
6.	Belgium	3.0	3.6	3.7	5.1	5.0
	EUR 12	2.4	3.4	3.6	4.7	. .
7.	UK	2.1	3.2	3.6	4.1	4.6
8.	Italy	1.7	3.2	3.1	3.8	4.3
9.	Ireland	1.5	2.0	2.2	2.6	2.9
10.	Spain	1.0	1.6	1.8	2.5	3.0
11.	Portugal	0.4	0.8	0.9	1.4	2.2
12.	Greece	0.5	0.8	0.9	1.2	1.6

Notes: Figures are rounded to one decimal point
Sources: EUROSTAT, *Social Portrait of Europe*, 1996: p.131 and *Social Expenditure and Receipts – 1980-94*, 1996, pp.21-23

Table A.3
Taxes and Social Security Contributions as % of GDP, 1975-95
Europe, USA, Canada, Japan and Australia in order of rank all for 1995

Rank	Country	1975	1980	1985	1989	All	1995 House*	Corp*
1.	Denmark	41	45	49	51	51	30	3
2.	Sweden	44	50	50	56	50	20	3
3.	Belgium	40	42	46	45	46	15	3
4.	Finland	35	33	36	43	46	17	1
5.	Luxemburg	. .	. .	. .	50	46	. .	. .
6.	France	37	42	46	44	45	7	2
7.	Netherlands	44	46	45	45	44	11	4
8.	Austria	39	42	43	41	42	12	2
9.	Greece	25	28	34	34	42*	4	4
10.	Norway	44	50	49	42	42	13	4
11.	Germany	40	41	41	41	39	10	2
12.	Ireland	. .	. .	39	36	35	. .	. .
13.	UK	36	36	38	36	35	10	3
14.	Switzerland	30	30	32	31	34	13	1
15.	Spain	. .	. .	29	35	34	. .	. .
16.	Portugal	. .	. .	. .	. .	34	. .	. .
17.	Canada	32	30	30	35	36*	15	3
18.	Australia	28	29	30	31	31	12	4
19.	United States	27	29	29	29	32*	11	3
20.	Japan	23	26	28	30	28*	7	4

Notes: * = 1994 not 1995
House = Household income taxes
Corp. = Corporate income taxes
Sources: CSO, *Economic Trends*, December 1987, p. 88 and November 1996, pp. 21, 22, 23 and 24.

Table A.4
Social Security Contributions as % of GNP, 1984 and 1994
Europe, USA, Canada, and Japan ranked in order of total at 1994

Country	Total contributions 1984	1994	Paid by employer 1984	1994
Netherlands	21	20	8	3
France	19	19	12	12
Germany	16	17	7	8
Finland	9	16	9	12
Belgium	15	16	9	9
Sweden	13	14	13	13
Italy	12	13	9	9
Spain	. .	13	. .	. .
Austria	12	13	10	10
Greece	11	13	. .	. .
Switzerland	9	11	3	4
UK	7	6	4	3
Japan	8	9	4	5
United States	7	7*	4	4*
Canada	3	6	3	5

Notes: * = 1989
Sources: CSO, *Economic Trends*, November 1996

Table A.5
Unit Labour Costs
European Countries, USA and Japan, 1980, 1991 and 1997
Countries ranked by highest relative costs in 1997 (relative to 19 industrial countries: US$ 1991 in each country)

Country	1980	1991	1997
Greece	101.8	100	121.4
Portugal	83.3	100	114.3
Austria	92.1	100	108.6
Germany	112.5	100	108.3
Belgium	117.2	100	106.9
Denmark	105.6	100	106.3
France	123.9	100	106.2
Netherlands	126.8	100	105.3
EUR 15 (relative to 6 non-EU countries)	118.3	100	96.0
Sweden	102.4	100	92.6
Ireland	111.2	100	91.1
Spain	99.2	100	86.4
UK	100.3	100	86.3
Italy	76.0	100	82.3
Finland	78.9	100	77.6
United States	99.4	100	106.0
Japan	80.3	100	112.8

Source: EC, *European Economy: Annual Economic Report for 1997*, Brussels, 1997: Table 35, pp. 260-1

Table A.6
Labour Costs in Industry and Services, 1981 and 1988
Direct and Indirect Costs as % of Total
European Countries, ranked by highest industry indirect costs 1988

	Direct				Indirect			
	Industry		Services		Industry		Services	
Country	1981	1988	1981	1988	1981	1988	1981	1988
France	71	69	70	68	29	31	30	32
Italy	75	71	71	69	25	29	29	31
Belgium	77	71	79	70	23	29	21	30
Netherlands	74	74	81	79	26	26	19	21
Portugal	74	74	78	77	26	26	22	23
Spain	75	75	75	75	25	25	25	25
EURO 12	78	76	78	77	22	24	22	23
Germany	79	77	79	77	21	23	21	23
Greece	81	80	78	79	19	20	22	21
Ireland	84	82	82	80	16	18	18	20
Luxemburg	86	84	87	87	14	16	13	13
UK	82	86	84	85	18	14	16	15

Notes: Direct costs = wages, bonuses, days not worked and benefits in kind
Indirect costs = statutory and non-statutory social security, vocational training and other services
Sources: EUROSTAT. *Social Portrait of Europe*, 1997: p.111

Table A.7
Total Labour Costs, Industry and Services (000 ECUs per month)
European Countries, 1981 and 1988 ranked by industry total costs in 1988

Country	Manufacturing 1981	1988	Services 1981	1988
Denmark	1.5	2.5	1.7	3.0
Netherlands	1.5	2.3	1.7	2.5
Belgium	1.6	2.2	2.2	2.8
Ireland	0.9	2.2	1.2	2.3
France	1.4	2.2	1.8	2.6
Germany	1.4	2.2	1.8	2.7
Luxemburg	1.5	2.1	1.8	2.8
Italy	1.0	2.0	1.7	3.2
EURO 12	1.3	1.8	1.6	2.5
UK	1.2	1.7	1.4	2.1
Spain	. .	1.4	. .	1.1
Greece	0.6	0.8	0.8*	1.7
Portugal	. .	0.5	. .	1.0

Notes: * = 1984
Sources: EUROSTAT, *Social Portrait of Europe*, 1996: pp.108-9

Table A.8
Usual Hours Worked per week, 1991
European Countries, ranked by proportion over 44
(percentage of employees, men and women)

Country	Under 35	36-39	40-44	45-48	Over 48
UK	10	29	29	12	20
Portugal	16	5	53	22	4
Ireland	12	30	42	6	10
Greece	10	22	52	10	6
EURO 12	7	43	35	7	8
France	7	68	15	4	6
Italy	9	81	55	7	3
Germany	1	83	7	2	7
Denmark	2	83	6	3	6
Spain	5	12	75	4	4
Luxemburg	3	2	91	2	2
Belgium	8	65	23	3	1
Netherlands	4	54	39	1	2

Notes: the longest hours were in agriculture – over 50 in the UK and Ireland, and 46 in Greece and Luxemburg. There was little difference between industry and services in any country
Sources: EUROSTAT, *Saocial Portrait of Europe*, 1996: p.121

Table A.9
Economic Activity and Income Support
UK Districts, ranked by high proportions on income support, 1993

District	Economic Activity rate %	% Receiving Income support
ENGLAND	62.7	15
Hackney	57.5	37
Tower Hamlets	51.9	35
Newham	54.5	33
Haringey	58.2	32
Manchester	50.8	32
Southwark	64.4	29
Lambeth	64.7	28
Islington	63.8	27
Brent	61.5	26
Hull	58.5	26
Greenwich	62.5	25
Merseyside	54.0	25
North Norfolk	56.3	25
Birmingham	59.3	24
Middlesborough	55.6	24
Camden	65.8	24
Lewisham	62.7	24
Waltham Forest	61.8	24
Leicester	58.3	23
Nottingham	55.9	23
Hartlepool	41.7	22
Sandwell	57.9	22
Wolverhampton	60.7	22
Merthyr	66.9	22
Hastings	67.3	21
Newcastle/Tyne	54.0	21
Barking	59.2	21
Hammersmith	64.8	21
Grimsby	65.0	21
Rhondda, Rhymney, Cynon	51.5	20
Blackburn	59.9	20
Salford	54.2	20
Halton	57.6	20
Coventry	62.6	20
Thanet	60.9	20
Wear Valley	48.3	20
Sunderland	60.4	20

Sources: CSO, *Regional Trends*, 1995, HMSO, Table 15.3, pp. 220 ff.

Table A.10
Umemployed and Social Protection, 1980, 1990, 1994
European Countries in order of unemployment rate, 1990 and USA and Japan
(Social Protection = expenditure as % of GDP)

Country	Unemployment Rate				Social Protection		
	1980	*1990*	*1994*		*1980*	*1990*	*1994*
Luxemburg	2.4	1.7	3.2		26.5	22.5	24.9
Sweden	2.2	1.8	9.8		. .	. .	. .
Austria	1.9	3.2	3.8		. .	. .	30.2
Finland	5.2	3.4	18.4		25.4	27.6	30.5
Portugal	7.6	4.6	7.0		12.8	15.0	19.5
Germany	2.7	4.8	9.1		28.8	26.9	30.8
Netherlands	6.4	6.2	7.2		30.1	32.2	32.3
Greece	2.7	6.4	8.9		9.7	16.1	16.0
Belgium	7.4	6.7	10.0		28.0	26.9	27.0
UK	5.6	7.0	9.6		21.5	22.7	28.1
EUR 15	5.8	7.7	11.3	EUR 12	24.3	25.2	27.6
Denmark	5.2	7.7	8.2		28.7	29.8	33.7
France	6.2	9.0	12.3		25.4	27.6	30.5
Italy	7.1	9.1	11.4		19.4	23.6	25.3
Ireland	8.0	13.4	14.3		20.6	19.4	21.1
Spain	11.6	16.2	24.1		18.1	20.7	23.6
USA	7.1	5.5	6.1		. .	. .	. .
Japan	2.0	2.1	2.9		. .	. .	. .

Sources: Unemployment rates from EC, *European Economy: Annual Report for 1997*, Brussels, 1997, Table 3, pp. 196-7
Social Protection from EUROSTAT, *Social Protection Expenditure and Receipts, 1980-94*, Table B 1., pp. 16-17

Table A.11
Old Age and Survivors Benefits, 1980 and 1990-3
European Countries, in order of over 60s as % of population, 1990

Country	Over 60s as % of population, 1990	Benefits as % of GDP 1980	Benefits as % of GDP 1993	Basic 1993 proportion (%)
Sweden	23	. .	. .	. .
Norway	21	. .	. .	. .
Belgium	20	10.7	11.4*	90
UK	20	8.7	10.4	65
Denmark	20	10.0	10.6	83
Germany	20	11.9	10.3	90
Italy	20	9.9	15.4	94
Austria	20	. .	. .	. .
Switzerland	19	. .	. .	. .
EURO 12	19 (1980 = 18)	8.6	9.1	89
Greece	19	6.1	8.7	87
Luxemburg	18	12.3	11.3	98
France	18	10.5	12.6	95
Spain	17	6.7	9.5	92
Finland	17	. .	. .	. .
Portugal	17	4.6	7.0	93
Netherlands	16	9.0	11.9	84
Ireland	15	7.3	5.6	72

Notes: Benefits include all payments on account of old age or retirement, redundancy etc. 'Basic' proportion includes both state payment and compulsory requirements, but not voluntary private schemes.
*Belgium = 1992, not 1993
Sources: Population: EUROSTAT, *Social Portrait of Europe*, Bsrussels, 1996: pp.14
Benefits: EUROSTAT, *Digest of Statistics on Social Protection in Europe: Old Age and Survivors: An Update*, Brussels, 1996, pp.144-5

Table A.12
Number of Persons in Receipt of Invalidity Pensions
Euriopean Countries, 1980 and 1991, in alphabetical order
Numbers in thousands of persons, male and female

Country	Drawing invalidity pension 1980	Drawing invalidity pension 1992	Drawing disabled all'ces 1980	Drawing disabled all'ces 1992	Total % Increase 1980-92	Drawing war pensions 1980	Drawing war pensions 1992
Belgium	251	247	98	179	23	447	359
Denmark*	168	253	. .	. .	. .	. .	. .
Germany	2,129	2,141	4,370	5,372	15	940	604
Greece	227	320	. .	74	70	54	39
Spain	1,027	1,603	5	330	85	. .	. .
France	422	559	357	533	40	644	456
Ireland	19	34	88	81	10	. .	. .
Italy	5,390	4,360	373	1,394	0	352	262
Netherlands	. .	. .	660	901	35	. .	. .
Portugal	401	469	16	52	25	. .	. .
UK	616	1,278	318	430	88	273	192

Notes: * = The Danish figure is for persons drawing early retirement
Sources: EUROSTAT, *Disabled Persons Statistical Data*, Brussels, 1995 Ch.1, Table 2.A, pp 123-129

Table A.13
Family Benefit % of GDP and per head, and means tested proportion
European Countries, 1980, 1990 and 1994,
Countries in order of ECU per head in 1994

| Country | ECU Per Capita | | | % of GDP | | | % means tested |
	1980	1990	1994	1980	1990	1994	1990
Denmark	253	583	771	2.7	2.9	3.7	2
Luxemburg	182	425	606	2.0	2.3	3.4	0
France	227	364	455	2.6	2.2	2.8	8
Germany	237	351	434	2.5	1.9	2.9	23
Belgium	267	331	365	3.1	2.2	2.3	0
UK	155	273	306	2.3	2.0	2.4	37
EUR 12	148	233	286	2.1	1.6	2.0	13
Netherlands	226	257	282	2.6	1.7	1.9	16
Ireland	82	251	273	2.0	2.6	0.7	42
Italy	56	97	113	1.0	0.6	0.7	16
Portugal	16	39	50	0.9	0.8	1.2	18
Spain	19	12	28	0.5	0.1	0.2	19
Greece	13	11	13	0.4	0.2	0.2	0

Notes: Benefits include cash for children, family and dependents and benefits in kind for accommodation etc.
Sources: EUROSTAT, *Digest of Statistics on Social Protection in Europe*, vol. 4., Faamily, 1993, pp. 78-81 and *Social Expenditure and Receipts, 1980-94*, 1996, p/ 53

Table A.14
Maternity Benefit, 1980 and 1991
European Countries, in order of highest payments in 1991
ECU per birth, 1980 and 1991 and % of GDP, 1980 and 1991

| Country | ECU per birth | | % of GDP | | % in cash |
	1980	1991	1980	1991	1991
Denmark	2,136	9,593	0.26	0.52	95
Luxemburg	3,274	7.018	0.31	0.39	80
France	1,683	4,927	0.52	0.41	56
UK	1,683	4,239	0.33	0.39	18
Belgium	1,079	3,031	0.16	0.24	76
EURO 12	1,566	3,002	0.30	0.26	50
Germany	1,723	2,954	0.26	0.20	91
Italy	630	1,704	0.12	0.12	100
Netherlands	737	1,635	0.11	0.13	50
Ireland	799	1,619	0.43	0.33	24
Spain	659	1,472	0.25	0.20	25
Portugal	173	573	0.13	0.14	71
Greece	202	371	0.10	0.10	60

Notes: Different European countries have different ways of paying for medical and hospital services
Sources: EUROSTAT, *Digest of Statistics on Social Protection in Europe, vol. 6 Maternity*, Brussels 1995, pp. 52-3

Annexe Two:
Case Studies

Over 400 people responded to a questionnaire circulated by Ken Coates MEP in December 1997 to Labour Party members in his North Nottinghamshire and Chesterfield Constituency. Here is a selection of the responses he received on disability and other welfare benefits.

A former miner from Mansfield
... I worked in the mining industry from the age of fifteen until 1982, when I was 39. I was involved in a bad accident which in the following 2 years resulted in 5 operations, after which I was declared unfit to go back to work, and was given incapacity retirement. My condition has deteriorated steadily since then. I have had over 20 medicals in Mansfield for the DSS ... I got mobility allowance awarded in 1985 for life and in January 1997 I passed the Tory all work test and received the paperwork which stated that my condition was expected to last for the rest of my life, and would therefore require no more medical certificates from my doctor. If the new plans go ahead, will this be accepted on behalf of New Labour, or will I be required to go again for a new medical? ... I know you've been under a lot of pressure lately, but please stick to your guns and principles. Believe you me, you will have more support than you think from traditional Labour voters.

A man from Newark whose Disability Living Allowance was withdrawn under the Benefit Integrity Project
'It is with deep regret that I feel I can no longer remain a member of the Labour Party as a direct result of the handling of myself and the disabled of this country. On Thursday of last week I received three letters, two from the DSS and on from Motability Finance Ltd. The point of these letters was to tell me that I was no longer entitled to

Disability Living Allowance . . . The reason given for stopping my benefit is because they said in 1995 I had a successful heart and lung transplant. In fact I had a heart, lung and liver transplant . . . it is far from a normal life. Most of us would like to get in to some sort of work wherever possible but this cannot be achieved by taking away our benefits first.' (from his resignation letter to Tony Blair, 14.12.97).

'. . . It deeply saddened me to have to disassociate myself from the Labour Party as I have for many years believed in its principles, many of which seem to have been abandoned by the present government. It worries me to think this could be the end of the Labour Party as we know it. Although I am no longer a party member I wish to offer my support in whatever course you decide to take.' (letter to Ken Coates).

A woman in Chesterfield whose daughter also lost all her DLA as a result of the Benefit Integrity Project

'. . . My youngest daughter was 16 last November and has had her mobility allowance taken away, despite the fact that she still needs it. So I have had to go into debt to buy a car as we definitely need transport. Good luck in your campaign. If I win the lottery I'll give you some money towards your aim.'

An unemployed man from the Newark area

'. . . I have been unemployed for some time and recently broke my hip in an accident. Every time the mortgage interest rates go up I have to pay the difference because social security interest payments do not rise immediately, leaving you to pay the difference, which can be for months. I was told in December that the shortfall was £22 a month, or £5.50 per week, which has to come out of my £117 per week income support. I now hear that it is being proposed to only pay the A Band in Council Tax for people on income support. In my case this would mean selling my house and moving. I might add that we haven't had a holiday for 12 years and no heating for 2 years. I cannot even afford calcium tablets to help with my broken hip recovery.

I thought with a Labour Government in, the stress of worrying whether you'd have a roof over your head would recede, but no, it seems to be picking up momentum. Is it necessary to have a revolution before the working classes get fair play?'

A man from the Chesterfield area

'I am a longstanding member of the Labour Party and of the Christian Socialist Movement . . . I also backed the amendment of Clause Four . . . I share the sense of despair to which you refer in your letter . . . I have spoken to others who are similarly distressed. Some of these people are recent converts who did not vote for us in 1992 but did so in 1997 . . . What I cannot stomach are the continued attacks on teachers by Stephen Byers which are ill-informed, and the benefit cuts which are shameful . . . The justification given for the benefit cuts is the so-called 'New Deal'. I'm afraid this has not been properly thought out. Attention needs to be paid to the *reasons* why people who are sick or disabled, lone parents and the unemployed, cannot get work . . . It needs to be optional, not compulsory.'

A woman in Bestwood Village, Nottingham

'Having believed in, and therefore supported (in many ways) the Labour Party of John Smith RIP, prior to May 1st 1997, I now feel betrayed by 'New' Labour and their efforts and intentions to abandon all previous principles. I've supported Labour for the exact same reasons as in your correspondence, and should they not revert back to their original principles, I cannot continue my Party membership. I feel too ashamed to be a part of such actions.'

A single mother in Whitwell, Bolsover

As a single parent with 3 children I have recently completed a college diploma and was considering a degree course. Under New Labour's legislation on grants and benefit cuts, I would find this extremely difficult. I think New Labour is the same as Old Tory and have now withdrawn my Labour Party membership.

A disabled woman in Walkeringham, Bassetlaw

I am slightly disabled and cannot work. Last year I was taken off disability. I went straight to my doctor and was given a sick note. This was refused by the DSS. I then put in an appeal which, after 6 very stressful months, I won. I am now back on disability, but I wonder what all the people worse than I am did at Christmas with all the worry and stress of the recent plans of the Labour Party.